Personal Best

B1 Pre-intermediate

Student's Book and Workbook combined edition **B**

Series Editor
Jim Scrivener

Student's Book Authors
Bess Bradfield with
Graham Fruen

Workbook Authors
Elizabeth Walter and
Kate Woodford

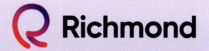

STUDENT'S BOOK CONTENTS

		LANGUAGE			SKILLS	
		GRAMMAR	PRONUNCIATION	VOCABULARY		
7	**City living**	▪ present perfect with *yet* and *already* ▪ present perfect with *for* and *since*	▪ *just* and *yet* ▪ *for* and *since*	▪ city features ▪ transportation	**LISTENING** ▪ a video about commuting around the world ▪ listening for facts and figures ▪ final /t/ sound	**WRITING** ▪ writing an essay ▪ giving opinions **PERSONAL BEST** ▪ an opinion essay about a problem
7A	Life in the city p58					
7B	The daily commute p60					
7C	A life in three cities p62					
7D	I think it's a great idea! p64					
8	**Food for thought**	▪ *too, too many, too much,* and *(not) enough* ▪ *have to, not have to,* and *can't*	▪ *too much sugar* ▪ sentence stress	▪ food and drink ▪ adjectives to describe food	**READING** ▪ an article about a course offered by a Gelateria in Bologna ▪ scanning for specific information ▪ linkers to contrast information (*although, but, however*)	**SPEAKING** ▪ sounding polite ▪ making and responding to invitations **PERSONAL BEST** ▪ making plans to go out with a friend
8A	Sweet, but dangerous p66					
8B	Ice cream university p68					
8C	You have to eat your vegetables! p70					
8D	First dates p72					
7 and **8**	**REVIEW** and **PRACTICE** p74					
9	**Money and shopping**	▪ *used to* ▪ the passive: simple present and past	▪ *used to/use to* ▪ sentence stress	▪ money verbs ▪ shopping	**LISTENING** ▪ a video about the importance of shopping centers ▪ identifying attitude and opinion ▪ filler expressions	**WRITING** ▪ writing a formal e-mail ▪ noun forms of verbs **PERSONAL BEST** ▪ an e-mail complaining about a purchase
9A	He used to be poor p76					
9B	What a bargain! p78					
9C	Going, going, gone! p80					
9D	I'd like a refund! p82					
10	**Sports and fitness**	▪ past perfect ▪ reported speech	▪ *'d* and *hadn't* ▪ weak form of *that*	▪ sports and competitions ▪ parts of the body	**READING** ▪ an article about wheelchair rugby ▪ finding information in a text ▪ giving examples	**SPEAKING** ▪ being helpful ▪ making inquiries **PERSONAL BEST** ▪ asking for information about a service or product
10A	Winning is everything! p84					
10B	Rock 'n' roll on wheels p86					
10C	He said it had changed his life p88					
10D	Could you tell me …? p90					
9 and **10**	**REVIEW** and **PRACTICE** p92					
11	**At home**	▪ *-ing*/infinitive verb patterns ▪ articles (*a/an, the,* no article)	▪ sentence stress ▪ *the*	▪ household items ▪ housework ▪ words to describe materials and clothes	**LISTENING** ▪ A video about what we really think of housework ▪ understanding and interpreting information ▪ omission of words	**WRITING** ▪ making writing interesting ▪ adjective order **PERSONAL BEST** ▪ writing an interesting description of a house
11A	Dream home p94					
11B	The truth about housework p96					
11C	Technology you can wear p98					
11D	House exchange p100					
12	**People and relationships**	▪ defining relative clauses ▪ uses of the *-ing* form and the infinitive	▪ sentence stress ▪ word stress	▪ relationships ▪ relationship verbs	**READING** ▪ an infographic showing how much time we spend on different activities ▪ interpreting data ▪ expressing approximate quantities	**SPEAKING** ▪ responding modestly ▪ saying thanks **PERSONAL BEST** ▪ thanking someone for a favor
12A	Bring your parents to work p102					
12B	In our lifetime p104					
12C	Long-distance love p106					
12D	Thanks a million! p108					
11 and **12**	**REVIEW** and **PRACTICE** p110					

Grammar practice p124　　Vocabulary practice p148　　Communication practice p162　　Irregular verbs p175

2　　Language App, unit-by-unit grammar and vocabulary games

WORKBOOK CONTENTS

		LANGUAGE			**SKILLS**	
		GRAMMAR	PRONUNCIATION	VOCABULARY		
7 City living **7A** p38 **7B** p39 **7C** p40 **7D** p41		▪ present perfect with *yet* and *already* ▪ present perfect with *for* and *since*	▪ *just* and *yet* ▪ *for* and *since*	▪ city features ▪ transportation	LISTENING ▪ listening for facts and figures	WRITING ▪ writing an essay
7 — REVIEW and PRACTICE			p42			
8 Food for thought **8A** p44 **8B** p45 **8C** p46 **8D** p47		▪ *too, too many, too much* and *(not) enough* ▪ *have to, not have to,* and *can't*	▪ *too much sugar* ▪ sentence stress	▪ food and drink ▪ adjectives to describe food	READING ▪ scanning for specific information	SPEAKING ▪ making and responding to invitations
8 — REVIEW and PRACTICE			p48			
9 Money and shopping **9A** p50 **9B** p51 **9C** p52 **9D** p53		▪ *used to* ▪ the passive	▪ *used to/use to* ▪ sentence stress	▪ money verbs ▪ shopping	LISTENING ▪ identifying attitude and opinion	WRITING ▪ writing a formal e-mail
9 — REVIEW and PRACTICE			p54			
10 Sports and fitness **10A** p56 **10B** p57 **10C** p58 **10D** p59		▪ past perfect ▪ reported speech	▪ *'d / hadn't* ▪ weak form of *that*	▪ sports and competitions ▪ parts of the body	READING ▪ finding information in a text	SPEAKING ▪ making inquiries
10 — REVIEW and PRACTICE			p60			
11 At home **11A** p62 **11B** p63 **11C** p64 **11D** p65		▪ *-ing*/infinitive verb patterns ▪ articles	▪ sentence stress ▪ *the*	▪ household items ▪ housework ▪ words to describe materials and clothes	LISTENING ▪ understanding and interpreting information	WRITING ▪ making writing interesting
11 — REVIEW and PRACTICE			p66			
12 People and relationships **12A** p68 **12B** p69 **12C** p70 **12D** p71		▪ restrictive relative clauses ▪ uses of the *-ing* form and the infinitive	▪ sentence stress ▪ word stress	▪ relationships ▪ relationship verbs	READING ▪ interpreting data	SPEAKING ▪ saying thanks
12 — REVIEW and PRACTICE			p72			

Writing practice **p77**

3

UNIT 7 City living

LANGUAGE present perfect with *yet* and *already* ■ city features

7A Life in the city

1 Discuss the questions in pairs.
1 Do you live in a city, a town, or a village?
2 Do you like where you live?
3 What are the good and bad things about it?

2 A Look at the picture. Which city is it?

B Match the words in the box with the things in the city.

| sidewalk   traffic lights   bridge |
| bike lane   crosswalk   bench |

1 _____ 2 _____ 3 _____ 4 _____ 5 _____ 6 _____

Go to Vocabulary practice: city features, page 148

3 A Read the text. Who is more positive about the city: Alex or Megan? _____

B Read the text again and match the headings in the box with the paragraphs.

| Cost of living   Job opportunities   The weather   The people   Transportation   Entertainment |

Big City

San Francisco is one of the fastest growing cities in the U.S. Today, we speak to two people who recently moved here and find out their first impressions of living in the city.

Alex, 25, is an IT professional. He just moved to San Francisco from London.

1 _____
There are so many tech companies here; it's really exciting. I've joined a networking group to meet people from the industry, and I've already been to a couple of events. Have I found a job yet? No … but I'm sure I will soon! At least I have my visa!

2 _____
In my apartment building, there are people of all nationalities, as well as from other places in the U.S. I haven't met all my neighbors yet, but I love living in a city where everyone is different.

3 _____
Whatever you're interested in, there's always something going on. I've already been to the theater twice and I've seen a baseball game, and I only arrived two weeks ago!

Megan, 27, has moved to San Francisco from her hometown in Idaho to study engineering.

4 _____
San Francisco is expensive and you need a good salary to live here. I've rented a room in a shared house, but after I've paid the rent, it doesn't leave me with much money for other things.

5 _____
All my friends told me that the summers wouldn't be as hot as back home. It hasn't been too cold yet, but it can get really foggy, especially when you're near the ocean.

6 _____
The traffic here is terrible, so forget driving! Cable cars are fun, but public transportation can get really crowded, so I just bought myself a bike. It's one of the best ways to get around the city, and the bike lanes are great.

present perfect with *yet* and *already* ■ city features **LANGUAGE** **7A**

4 **A** Who said sentences 1–3: Alex or Megan?
1 Have I found a job _____?
2 It hasn't been too cold _____ .
3 I've _____ been to the theater twice.

B Complete the sentences with the words in the box. Check your answers in the text.

already   yet (x2)

5 Answer the questions about the sentences in exercise 4. Then read the Grammar box.
1 Which tense is used in the sentences? _____
2 Which word do we add in questions and negative sentences to talk about something we expected to happen before now? _____
3 Which word do we add to sentences to talk about something that happened earlier than we expected? _____

> **Grammar** present perfect with *yet* and *already*
>
> Something that happened earlier than we expected: *He's **already** finished his homework.*
> Something we expected to happen before now: ***Have** you **had** lunch **yet**? I **haven't seen** the movie **yet**.*

Go to Grammar practice: present perfect with *yet* and *already* page 124

6 **A** ▶7.3 **Pronunciation:** *just* and *yet* Listen and repeat the words. Pay attention to the /y/ sound (*yet*) and the /ǰ/ sound (*just*).
1 /y/ **y**et **y**oung **y**ou us**u**ally
2 /ǰ/ **j**ust **j**ob **g**ym bri**dge**

B ▶7.4 How do you say the sentences? Listen, check, and repeat.
1 Have **y**ou **j**oined a **g**ym **y**et?
2 She **j**ust **u**sed a **y**ellow pen.
3 I already have a **j**ob.
4 An**g**ela hasn't arrived **y**et.

Go to Communication practice: Student A, page 162; Student B, page 170

7 ▶7.5 Complete the phone conversation between Alex and his friend Josh. Use the present perfect form of the verbs in the box and *yet* or *already*. Listen and check.

find   make   meet   not see   go

Josh Hi Alex, this is Josh. How's it going in San Francisco?
Alex Great, thanks. I'm really enjoying it.
Josh Have you ¹_____ any friends ²_____ ?
Alex Yes, I ³_____ quite a few people. As a matter of fact, I just had lunch with two guys who work for an Internet company.
Josh Great! And ⁴_____ you _____ a job ⁵_____ ?
Alex No, not ⁶_____ . But I ⁷_____ on three interviews. I'm waiting to hear back from them.
Josh Well, good luck! Oh, what's Chinatown like?
Alex I ⁸_____ it ⁹_____ ! I've been too busy, but I might go this weekend.

8 **A** Make a list of things you have already done and things you still have to do this week.

B In pairs, ask and answer the question *Have you ... yet?* about your partner's list. Give more information in your answers.
A *Have you been to the supermarket yet?*
B *Not yet. I'm going shopping tonight, though.*
A *Have you called your parents yet?*
B *Yes, I've already called them twice this week.*

Things to do
– go to the supermarket
– call my parents
– get together with my friends

Personal Best Write about the town or city you live in.

7 SKILLS LISTENING listening for facts and figures ■ final /t/ sound ■ transportation

7B The daily commute

1 Is traffic a problem in your town/city? How do most people get to work?

2 Look at the pictures in exercise 4. In pairs, use the words in the box to describe them.

> traffic jam   drive   rush hour   commuter   passenger   parking lot
> platform   take the train   parking space   public transportatiton

In picture a, people are driving to work, but there's a really bad traffic jam.

Go to Vocabulary practice: transportation, page 148

3 7.8   Look at exercise 4. Which cities do pictures a–c show? Watch or listen to the first part of *Learning Curve* and check.

a _____   b _____   c _____

Skill   listening for facts and figures

We often have to listen for specific information.
- Before you listen, focus on what type of information you need to listen for. For example, is it a number, a person, a time, a place, etc.?
- Listen for "clues." For example, if the information is an age, you might hear "old" or "years."
- Write the exact word(s) you hear. Then read the sentences to make sure they make sense.

4 A Read the Skill box. Match the types of information in the box with the blanks in the text.

> a specific time   a verb (x2)   a noun   an adjective (x2)   a period of time (x2)   a number (x2)

B ▶7.8   Watch or listen again and complete the text with the correct words.

Commuting around the world

The global average commuting time is ¹ _____ , but it is much worse in some cities.

The average travel time is
² _____ .

Rush hour is between ³ _____
and 9:30 in the morning.

This city has a population of
⁴ _____ people.

Companies employ "pushers" to
⁵ _____ passengers onto trains.

They wear ⁶ _____ gloves as
a sign of respect to passengers.

⁷ _____ passengers use the
train system every day.

Seven million ⁸ _____ come
into this city every day.

24% of people have ⁹ _____
about a parking space in the last
year.

Parking lots are so ¹⁰ _____
that people can lose their cars.

listening for facts and figures ■ final /t/ sound ■ transportation **LISTENING** SKILLS **7B**

5 ▶ 7.9 Watch or listen to the second part of the show. How do Mike, Sandra, and Lorena get to work/the university?

Mike

Sandra

Lorena

6 A Read questions 1–8. What kind of information do you need to answer them?
1 How long does Mike's commute take in total?   *a period of time*
2 What time does he usually leave the house?   _____
3 What causes him problems on his commute?   _____
4 Which city is Sandra in?   _____
5 How often does she usually travel with Bonnie?   _____
6 How far is it to Sandra's work?   _____
7 How long does it take Lorena to walk to the university?   _____
8 How much does she spend on public transportation?   _____

B ▶ 7.9 Watch or listen again. Answer the questions.

7 Discuss the questions in pairs.
1 How do you get to work/college/class?
2 How long does it take you?
3 What time do you start out?
4 Do you ever have any problems?
5 Who do you travel with?
6 How does the trip make you feel?

8 ▶ 7.10 Listen to the sentences from the show. When are the /t/ sounds in **bold** pronounced?
1 What time do you se**t** off?
2 My bigges**t** problem is pedestrians.
3 I'm here in fron**t** of our building in New York.
4 Today, I'm jus**t** listening to my car radio.

Listening builder final /t/ sound

English speakers don't often pronounce the /t/ sound at the end of a word when the next word begins with a consonant. If the next word begins with a vowel sound, they link the sounds together.
I get off the bus.   *I ge(t) to talk with my good friend.*
There's still a lot of traffic.   *She doesn'(t) drive.*

9 ▶ 7.11 Read the Listening builder. Listen and complete the sentences.
1 The _____ _____ to get to work is to drive, _____ _____ is impossible.
2 I _____ _____ at 8:00 and _____ _____ me over an hour.
3 The traffic _____ _____ completely, so we _____ _____ and walked.
4 It's the _____ _____ in the world for commuting, but they _____ _____ buy a car.
5 I _____ _____ taking the subway. I get _____ _____ _____ people come out of the station.

10 A In pairs, prepare a talk of 1–2 minutes about the transportation system in your city or country. Use the ideas in the boxes.

| the type of transportation people use | the cost and frequency of public transportation | the problems commuters have | suggestions for people visiting your city or country |

B Work with another pair. Take turns listening, then ask at least one question.

Personal Best Write a paragraph about the advantages and disadvantages of one type of transportation.

61

7 LANGUAGE present perfect with *for* and *since*

7C A life in three cities

1 A Look at the pictures. Try to answer the questions in pairs.
1 Who is the person?
2 What is her job?
3 What movies has she been in?
4 What nationality is she?

B Read the introduction in the text and check your answers.

A TALE OF THREE CITIES

She won an Oscar for her first movie, *12 Years a Slave*, in 2013. Since then, the Kenyan actress Lupita Nyong'o has become a Hollywood superstar and appeared on red carpets and magazine covers all over the world. We look at the three cities that have shaped this talented actress.

MEXICO CITY
Lupita was born in 1983 in Mexico City, where her father was working at a university. The family returned to Kenya when she was just a few months old, but at the age of 16, Lupita went back to Mexico for a year to learn Spanish. She's spoken Spanish since 1999, and has even given TV interviews in Spanish.

NAIROBI
Lupita went to school in Nairobi, and this is where she first started acting. Her first big performance was at the age of 14 when she played Juliet in *Romeo and Juliet*. One of her happiest memories is of climbing the mango trees in her grandmother's village and eating the fruit straight from the branches!

NEW YORK
Lupita has lived in Brooklyn, New York, since 2013, and this is now her home. When she's not working, she spends her time doing yoga and cooking her favorite dishes like *enchiladas verdes*. She also loves riding the subway into Manhattan to go shopping, just like anyone else in New York! The big question is: Where next for Lupita?

2 Read the rest of the text. Are the sentences true (T) or false (F)?
1 Lupita has been very famous since 2013. ____
2 She has had an interest in acting for over ten years. ____
3 She has spoken Spanish since she was a small child in Mexico. ____
4 She has lived in New York for most of her life. ____

3 Look at sentences 1–4 in exercise 2. Choose the correct options to answer the questions. Then read the Grammar box.
1 Are the situations in the sentences finished? *yes / no*
2 Which tense are the verbs in? *present continuous / present perfect*
3 When do we use the word *since*? *for a point in time / for a period of time*
4 When do we use the word *for*? *for a point in time / for a period of time*

Grammar present perfect with *for* and *since*

For situations that started in the past and continue in the present:
I**'ve worked** as an actress **for** twenty years.   She **hasn't seen** me **since** 2010.

Look! We use **for** for a period of time and **since** for a point in time:
I've had this car **for six months**.   I've had this car **since February**.

Go to Grammar practice: present perfect with *for* and *since*, page 125 present perfect with *for* and *since* **LANGUAGE 7C**

4 A ▶ 7.13 **Pronunciation:** *for* and *since* Listen and repeat the sentences. Pay attention to the rhythm. Are *for* and *since* stressed or unstressed words?

1 She's lived in New York since 2013.
2 She hasn't been to Mexico for a few years.

B ▶ 7.14 Underline the stressed words in the sentences. In pairs, practice saying them. Listen, check, and repeat.

1 I've lived in this house for six years.
2 She's known him since 1995.
3 I haven't seen him for months.
4 They've had the car since March.

Go to Communication practice: Student A, page 162; Student B, page 170

5 ▶ 7.15 Listen to the conversation and answer the questions.

1 Where do you think the people are?
2 How do Laura and Pete know each other?
3 What is Jess's job?
4 What do Laura and Jess discuss at the end?
5 Do you think connections are important for finding a good job?

6 A Complete the questions with the simple past or present perfect form of the verbs in parentheses.

1 Where _____ Laura and Pete _____? (meet)
2 How long _____ Jess _____ in L.A.? (be)
3 How long _____ Jess _____ in Toronto? (live)
4 How long _____ Jess _____ scripts for TV and movies? (write)
5 What _____ she _____ before she was a writer? (do)
6 How long _____ Laura and Pete _____ the idea for the TV comedy series? (have)

B ▶ 7.15 Listen to the conversation again. Ask and answer questions 1–6 in pairs.

7 A Complete the circles with information about you.

- the name of an important friend
- the name of your street
- your occupation (job/student, etc.)
- a hobby you enjoy
- an important possession
- a place you want to visit
- something you use every day
- something you are terrified of

B In pairs, ask and answer the question *How long have you ...?* with an appropriate verb and the information in the circles. Try to give more information.

A *How long have you known Martin?*
B *I've known him since we were in high school together. We were in the same class.*
A *How long have you had your phone?*
B *I've had it for six months. It was a birthday present from my brother.*

Personal Best Think of someone you know well and write a paragraph about his/her life. Try to use the present perfect with *for* and *since*.

7 SKILLS WRITING writing an essay ■ giving opinions

7D I think it's a great idea!

1 Look at the pictures in exercise 2. Discuss the questions in pairs.
1. How often do you use your cell phone each day?
2. Do you call people when you are on the street? If so, who?
3. Do you use your phone on public transportation? If so, what for?
4. Do you send messages when you go out with friends? If so, how often?
5. Do you think we use our phones too much? Why/Why not?

2 A Read the title of the essay. What does the verb *ban* mean?
a make something illegal ☐   b make something easier ☐

B Read the essay. Does Kai agree or disagree with the question?

Is it time to ban smartphones in public?
Kai Meng

Smartphones are amazing inventions and help us in lots of different ways, but I'm worried that we use them too much. Every day, I see hundreds of people using their phones in the city, and it's causing some serious problems.

First, I believe smartphones can be dangerous. When people are sending messages or listening to music with headphones while walking down the street, they don't concentrate on the traffic, and it's much easier for them to have an accident.

The second reason is that I think talking on phones in public is annoying. If you're on public transportation or in a restaurant, you don't want to hear someone else's conversation. In my opinion, people should wait to call their friends and colleagues in private, unless it's a real emergency.

Finally, banning smartphones in public is a good idea because it would make people more sociable and encourage them to talk more. Even when some people get together with their friends, they spend half the time checking their phones and going on social media. If they didn't have their phones, they'd talk to each other more, and they'd have a much better time.

In conclusion, although there are lots of advantages to smartphones, I think we should ban them in public. Personally, I think this would be safer for pedestrians, nicer for passengers on public transportation, and would help us communicate with each other more.

3 Answer the questions about the essay. Then read the Skill box.
1. How many reasons for banning smartphones does Kai give? What are they? Which paragraphs are they in?
2. What is the purpose of paragraph 1? *to introduce the topic / to summarize all his reasons*
3. What is the purpose of the final paragraph? *to introduce the topic / to summarize all his reasons*

🔧 Skill writing an essay

In essays, we discuss a topic and give our point of view.
- Organize your ideas into paragraphs (introduction, reasons, and conclusion).
- Explain the reasons for your opinions in separate paragraphs. Give examples or evidence to support them.
- Use sequencers, like *first*, *the second reason*, *finally*, and *in conclusion* to help readers.

writing an essay ■ giving opinions **WRITING** SKILLS **7D**

4 Look at the pictures. In pairs, think of some reasons why we *shouldn't* ban smartphones in public.

a

b

c

5 A Match the two columns to make sentences. Did you have similar ideas?

1 We can check e-mails, read documents,
2 I believe this is very important
3 Personally, I love being able to watch
4 In my opinion, smartphones
5 They make our lives safer, more
6 Second, smartphones make
7 In conclusion, I don't think we should
8 The first reason is that phones help us
9 The last reason is that they are
10 Modern technology has changed

a the way we communicate.
b have made our lives better in three different ways.
c stay in touch with each other.
d for our safety.
e us work more efficiently.
f and organize meetings outside the office.
g lots of fun and keep us entertained.
h movies or play games when I'm on the subway or a bus.
i ban smartphones in public.
j efficient, and even more fun.

B Which sentences can be found in:
the introduction? _____   paragraph 3? _____   the conclusion? _____
paragraph 2? _____   paragraph 4? _____

6 A In pairs, use the sentences in 5A to help you write an essay against banning smartphones in public.

B Which essay is more convincing: Kai's or the one you wrote in exercise 6A? Do you think we should or shouldn't ban smartphones in public?

7 Read the essay in exercise 2 again. Underline any phrases Kai uses to give his opinion.

Text builder | giving opinions

We use a variety of phrases to give our opinions:
I (don't) think/believe (that) …   I'm worried/delighted (that) …   … is a good/bad idea.
In my opinion/view, …   Personally, …   I would(n't) say (that) …

8 Read the Text builder. In pairs, give your opinions about ideas 1–5. Explain your ideas.
1 I *think / don't think* public transportation should be free for everyone because …
2 Children playing computer games is a *good / bad* idea because …
3 In my opinion, learning English *is / isn't* very difficult because …
4 Personally, I *watch / don't watch* too much TV because …
5 I *would / wouldn't* say that we eat less healthily than our parents because …

9 A PREPARE Choose an essay title and decide if you agree or disagree with it. Give three reasons with examples and evidence to support them.

• Should universities be free for everyone?
• Do we need to ban fast-food restaurants?
• Should people who live in cities be allowed to have pets?
• Do we need stores now that we can buy everything online?

B PRACTICE Write an essay giving your opinion. Use the Skill box and Text builder to help you.

C PERSONAL BEST Exchange essays with another student and correct any mistakes. Is his/her essay convincing? How could he/she improve it?

Personal Best Write an essay with the opposite point of view from the one in exercise 9.

65

UNIT 8

Food for thought

LANGUAGE *too, too many, too much,* and *(not) enough* ■ food and drink

8A Sweet, but dangerous

1 Put the words in the box in the correct columns. Can you add two more words to each column?

| beef | cabbage | peach | salmon | strawberry | shrimp | lamb | eggplant |

fruit	vegetables	meat	fish and seafood

Go to Vocabulary practice: food and drink, page 149

2 Ask and answer the questions in pairs.
1 What did you have for breakfast?
2 What did you have for dinner last night?
3 What food do you eat if you want a snack?
4 What would you cook for a romantic dinner?
5 Are you allergic to any food?
6 Do you think you have a healthy diet? Why/Why not?

3 Look at the picture of the breakfast. Do you think it's healthy? How much added sugar do you think it contains? Read the text and check.

Most of us know that too much sugar isn't good for us. We know that we shouldn't eat a lot of chocolate or drink too many soft drinks. But how much do we really know about the other kinds of food we eat?

Australian moviemaker, Damon Gameau, decided to investigate the "hidden" sugar in food. He spent 60 days eating only products advertised as "healthy," such as low-fat yogurt, cereal bars, fruit juices, and sports drinks. But instead of feeling healthier, Damon gained 8 kg. and started to have health problems. The reason? The high levels of sugar that manufacturers add to many food products to make them taste better. The breakfast pictured here looks good, but the juice, cereal, and yogurt actually contain a total of fourteen teaspoons of extra sugar!

Damon says that food companies are not honest enough about the amount of sugar they add to their products. Their marketing makes us believe we're eating and drinking well, when we really aren't. The World Health Organization recommends a daily limit of 25 g. (about six teaspoons) of sugar. That means there's enough sugar in three quarters of a can of cola for one day.
After Damon's experiment finished, he returned to his usual diet of fresh fruit, vegetables, meat, and fish. His weight came down and his health problems disappeared. He still enjoys a little chocolate once in a while, but he finds that most processed food now tastes too sweet.
So next time you're in the supermarket, remember to check how much sugar is in that "healthy" cereal before you buy it!

4 Check (✓) the best title for the article. Explain your answer.
1 Is sugar good or bad for you? ☐
2 How to lose weight in 60 days ☐
3 The truth about sugar and processed food ☐
4 Five unhealthy foods to avoid ☐

5 Discuss the questions in pairs.
1 Did the text surprise you? Why/Why not?
2 Do you think people in your country eat too much sugar?
3 How often do you check how much sugar is in the products you buy?
4 Should the government do anything about sugar in food? If so, what?

too, too many, too much, and *(not) enough* ■ food and drink **LANGUAGE 8A**

6 A Complete the sentences with the words in the box. Check your answers in the text.

| too   too much   too many   not   enough |

1 We shouldn't drink _____ soft drinks.
2 _____ sugar isn't good for us.
3 Food companies are _____ honest enough.
4 There's _____ sugar in three quarters of a can of cola for one day.
5 Most processed food tastes _____ sweet.

B Match the words from sentences 1–5 with the definitions. Then read the Grammar box.
1 too / too much / too many
2 enough
3 not enough

a less than necessary
b more than necessary
c the right amount

Grammar *too, too many, too much,* and *(not) enough*

More than necessary:
It's **too** noisy. I can't concentrate.
You put **too much** milk in my coffee!
There are **too many** people on the bus.

The right amount:
We have **enough** eggs to bake a cake.
Is the room warm **enough** for you?

Less than necessary:
I do**n't** have **enough** time.
The car is**n't** fast **enough**.
OR The car's **not** fast **enough**.

Go to Grammar practice: *too, too many, too much,* and *(not) enough*, page 126

7 A 8.3 **Pronunciation:** *too much sugar* Listen and repeat the sentence from the text. Pay attention to the sounds in **bold**: /uː/, /ə/, and /ʊ/.

T**oo** m**u**ch s**u**gar isn't good for us.

B 8.4 How do you say the words? Listen, check, and repeat.

c**oo**k   s**ou**p   c**u**p   f**oo**d   en**ou**gh   p**u**t   bl**oo**d   sh**ou**ld   **u**se

8 8.5 How do you say the questions? Listen, check, and repeat. Ask and answer the questions in pairs.
1 Do you have enough time to cook dinner every night?
2 Do you think good food is too expensive?
3 Do you spend too much time using social media sites?
4 Do you think you have too many clothes?
5 Is your Internet connection fast enough for you?
6 Do you know anyone who drinks too much coffee?

9 8.6 Listen to a conversation. Check (✓) the food that the restaurant needs to buy.

Go to Communication practice: Student A, page 162; Student B, page 170

10 A Complete the sentences with your own ideas. Compare them in pairs.
1 I don't spend enough time on _____ .
2 I spend too much money on _____ .
3 I worry about _____ too much.
4 Sometimes, I'm too _____ .
5 I have too many _____ .
6 I don't think I'm _____ enough.

B Tell the rest of the class about your partner.

He doesn't spend enough time on his homework.

Personal Best Write a list of ingredients for three of your favorite dishes.

67

SKILLS READING scanning for specific information ■ linkers to contrast information

8B Ice cream university

1 Look at the title of the article and the pictures. Discuss the questions in pairs.
1 Where do you think the university is?
2 Who do you think takes courses here?
3 Would you like to learn how to make ice cream?
4 What's your favorite flavor of ice cream?

> **Skill** scanning for specific information
>
> **To find a specific piece of information in a text quickly, you should scan for it.**
> • Identify the key word(s) in the question for the information you need.
> • Quickly look for the key words in the text. You can use your finger to help you.
> • Stop when you find the key word. If the information you need isn't there, continue scanning until the key word appears again.

2 Read the Skill box. Scan the text and answer the questions. The key words are underlined.
1 What is <u>gelato</u>?
2 When did the <u>museum</u> open?
3 How much does a <u>one-day course</u> cost?
4 When was the Gelato University <u>founded</u>?
5 What is the <u>average age</u> of students at the university?

3 <u>Underline</u> the key words in the questions. Scan the text again to answer them.
1 How many students attend the university every year?
2 What languages are classes taught in?
3 What happens if you make *gelato* using too much sugar?
4 What is the right temperature for *gelato*?
5 How much is a visit to the museum?

4 Read the text in detail. Match the headings in the box with the paragraphs A–E.

> The secret of good *gelato*   A city to study in   If you just want a taste
> A course for everyone   A mix of students

 Text builder linkers to contrast information

> **but:** There are courses that last up to five weeks, **but** I'm going to try the one-day course.
> **however:** There are courses that last up to five weeks. **However**, I'm going to try the one-day course.
> **although: Although** there are courses that last up to five weeks, I'm going to try the one-day course.
> I'm going to try the one-day course, **although** there are courses that last up to five weeks.

5 A Read the Text builder. <u>Underline</u> examples of *but*, *however,* and *although* in the text. In pairs, discuss what information is contrasted.

B Complete the sentences with *but*, *however,* and *although*. Which paragraphs do they go with?
1 _____ *gelato* is Italian, it has an international reputation.
2 It's a complicated process, _____ after a few hours, I have a liter of pink ice cream.
3 It's only four euros for children under thirteen. _____ , they have to be accompanied by an adult.
4 I'm really looking forward to this course, _____ I've never been a "good student."
5 There's even a course to become a professional *gelato* taster. _____ it sounds like a dream job, I don't think I could eat ice cream 365 days a year!

6 Discuss the questions in pairs.
1 Apart from English, are you studying anything else right now?
2 What courses would you like to take if you had the time and the money?
3 If you could start your own business, what would it be?

scanning for specific information ■ linkers to contrast information   READING   SKILLS   8B

ICE CREAM UNIVERSITY

A _____

The city of Bologna in Italy is home to the oldest university in the world. It was founded in 1088. The list of former students includes artists, politicians, poets, and even movie directors. However, what a lot of people don't realize is that Bologna is also home to another, much newer, university. I've signed up for a course, although I'm not going to study law or engineering. I'm going to learn how to make *gelato*, Italian ice cream. Welcome to Gelato University!

B _____

The Carpigiani Gelato University was founded in 2003, and every year it attracts more than 6,000 students who want to learn how to make perfect ice cream. However, it's not just about making ice cream. Students all have the same dream of starting their own *gelato* business, so classes include how to write a business plan, how to market your product, even how to design your own *gelateria*, or ice cream store. There are courses that last up to five weeks, but I'm going to try the one-day course, which costs about 100 euros.

C _____

In my class of 20, there are students from all over the world and, although my classes are in English, there are also classes in Italian, Spanish, Chinese, and other languages. The average age of the students is about 35, but company director Robert from L.A. is planning to go into the *gelato* business at the age of 72! "You're never too old to try new things," he says.

D _____

Back to the classroom, and today we're making strawberry *gelato*. However, before we start, there's a science class. There's a lot of chemistry and mathematics, and a calculator is essential. If there's too much sugar in the mixture, it won't freeze. If there's not enough air, it will be too heavy. And it has to be served at the right temperature (5–10° C), which is much warmer than normal ice cream.

E _____

If you're interested in *gelato*, but you don't have the time or money to take a course, the university also has its own Gelato Museum, opened in 2012. For five euros, you can visit the museum, discover the history of *gelato*, the technology behind it and, of course, taste some of the different flavors! And if you're wondering how my strawberry *gelato* tasted, it was delicious!

Personal Best — Write a paragraph about your school or college. Remember to use linkers to contrast information.

8 LANGUAGE
have to, not have to, and *can't* ■ adjectives to describe food

8C You have to eat your vegetables!

1 A ▶ 8.7 Look at the pictures of school lunches. Which countries do you think they are from? Listen and check.

a

b

c

B ▶ 8.7 Match the adjectives in the box with the pictures. Listen again and check.

healthy   crunchy   sweet   spicy   salty   tasty

Go to Vocabulary practice: adjectives to describe food, page 150

2 Discuss the questions in pairs.
1 Did you ever have school lunches? If so, what were they like?
2 Which dishes from your childhood did you love/hate? Why?

3 Look at the pictures. Do you recognize the man? In pairs, answer the questions. Read the text and check.
1 What is the man's job?
2 Which country was he in?
3 Why was he in this country?
4 Why does he look disappointed?

THE FOOD REVOLUTION THAT FAILED

British celebrity chef, Jamie Oliver, tasted failure for the first time with his American TV show, *Jamie's Food Revolution.* One of the biggest health problems in the U.S. is obesity, and Jamie thought he could help by changing what children ate … but he found that it wasn't so easy.

In the U.S., more than 32 million children eat in school cafeterias every day. Unfortunately, the meals aren't always very healthy, and some children don't have to eat fruit or vegetables. Instead, they can choose hamburgers and pizzas with sweet drinks, like chocolate milk.

In 2010 and 2011, Jamie conducted an experiment. He tried changing the menu at a school in Los Angeles. The cooks made different meals, including vegetarian curry, fresh salads, and spicy chicken noodles. However, Jamie's experiment failed, and most children threw his new recipes away. With hungry children and angry parents, hamburgers and pizzas were soon back on the menu.

However, it's not all bad news. Although Jamie's idea didn't work, things are changing. New laws say that all schools have to serve healthier food. School meals can't contain too much salt, and cafeterias have to offer two vegetables a day … but these things take time. According to some previous rules, tomato sauce on pizzas counted as "one vegetable"!

4 Discuss the questions in pairs.
1 What do you think about Jamie's experiment?
2 Why do you think it failed?
3 What would you think if he tried to change school meals in your country?

have to, not have to, and *can't* ■ adjectives to describe food   **LANGUAGE 8C**

5 A Match the two parts to make sentences. Check your answers in the text.
1 Children **don't have to**   a serve healthier food.
2 All schools **have to**   b eat fruit or vegetables.
3 School meals **can't**   c contain too much salt.

B Answer the questions about the words in **bold** in sentences 1–4. Then read the Grammar box.
1 Which words mean "there is a rule to do this"? _____
2 Which words mean "this is not necessary"? _____
3 Which word means "this is not allowed"? _____

> **Grammar**   *have to, not have to,* and *can't*
>
> **Obligation:**   **Not necessary:**   **Prohibition:**
> You **have to** start school at 9:00 a.m.   You do**n't have to** take the course,   Students **can't** use a calculator
> Do they **have to** wear a uniform?   but you can if you want.   during the exam.

Go to Grammar practice: *have to, not have to,* and *can't,* page 127

6 Choose the correct options to complete the hotel rules. Would you like to stay at this hotel? Why/Why not?

HOTEL RULES

1 Guests *have to / don't have to* pay an extra $8 if they want breakfast.
2 Guests *have to / can't* sit at the same table every day. The room numbers are on the tables.
3 Guests *don't have to / can't* choose the cooked breakfast. Cereal and toast are also available.
4 Guests *don't have to / have to* arrive for breakfast before 9:00 a.m. when the kitchen closes.
5 Guests *can't / don't have to* take any food to their rooms. This is not allowed.
6 Guests *can't / have to* check out before 10:00 a.m. or we will charge them for an extra day.

7 A ▶ 8.10 **Pronunciation: sentence stress** Listen to the sentences. <u>Underline</u> the stressed words.
1 People have to carry an identity card at all times.
2 You don't have to buy a ticket when you get on the bus.
3 People can't use their cell phones on public transportation.
4 Children have to stay in school until the age of 18.
5 Parents don't have to send their children to school. They can educate them at home.
6 Everyone has to vote in the national elections.

B ▶ 8.10 Say the sentences, paying attention to the stress in each one. Listen again, check, and repeat.

8 In pairs, decide if the sentences in exercise 7A are true in your country.

Go to Communication practice: Student A, page 163; Student B, page 171

9 A In pairs, imagine you are the managing director of a new company. Write a list of rules that will keep your employees happy and productive and make your company successful. Think about these factors:

working hours | meetings | food and drink | social activities | breaks during the day
days off / vacations | work clothes | communication

B Tell the rest of the class your rules.

Personal Best Write a list of rules in your place of work or college. How could you change them to make them better?

71

8 SKILLS SPEAKING making and responding to invitations ■ sounding polite

8D First dates

1 In pairs, look at the pictures of restaurants. Decide which are the best places for the situations in the box.

> a business meeting   a first date   getting together with friends
> a birthday celebration   lunch by yourself   a family meal

2 Discuss the questions in pairs.
1. How would you feel if you had a first date?
2. Where would you go on a first date?
3. Who would you ask for advice about a first date?

3 ▶ 8.11   Watch or listen to the first part of *Learning Curve*. Are the sentences true (T) or false (F)?
1. Jack feels shy about asking Eleanor out on a date. ____
2. Jack met Eleanor while he was studying at the university. ____
3. He invites Simon to try his new dish and he wants his advice. ____
4. Simon thinks Jack should take Eleanor to a fish-and-chips restaurant. ____
5. Jack rings Eleanor to ask her out on a date. ____

4 ▶ 8.11   Use the words in the box to complete what Jack and Simon said. Watch or listen again and check.

> dish   great   be   in   sounds
> new   Would   that   interested
> you   trying   a   Thanks   out

Conversation builder — making and responding to invitations

Inviting:
Would you like to ...?
Would you be interested in ...?
Do you want to ...?
Do you feel like ...?

Accepting:
I'd love to. Thank you.
Thanks, that sounds great!
That's very nice/kind of you.
That would be wonderful.
Fantastic.

Refusing:
That's really nice of you, but I'm sorry, I can't.
I'm afraid I already have plans.
I really appreciate the invitation, but ...
Sorry, I think I'm busy that evening.

5 Read the Conversation builder. In pairs, take turns inviting your partner for coffee one day this week. Refuse the first time, but when he/she invites you for coffee on a different day, accept.

making and responding to invitations ■ sounding polite **SPEAKING** **SKILLS** **8D**

6 A ▶ 8.12 Watch or listen to the second part of the show. Where do Jack and Eleanor decide to go for their date?

B ▶ 8.12 Complete the conversation with the words in the box. Watch or listen again and check.

appreciate like fancy sorry want kind

Jack   I was wondering if you'd ¹_____ having dinner with me at my restaurant?
Eleanor Oh, that's right, you're a chef. Thanks, that's very ²_____ of you.
Jack   Great. I know it's short notice, but would you ³_____ to come tonight? I have a new, special dish.
Eleanor Did you say tonight? That's really nice of you, but I'm ⁴_____, I can't. I already have plans.
Jack   Well, do you ⁵_____ to go out on the weekend? Perhaps tomorrow?
Eleanor Er, I would. I really ⁶_____ the invite, but, I'm going to go visit my granddad.

7 ▶ 8.13 Listen and repeat the phrases when you hear the beeps. Do Eleanor and Jack sound polite?

Skill sounding polite

It's important to sound polite in English, especially when you say something negative.
• Use intonation to express yourself. Flat intonation can sound rude.
• Apologize before you say something negative.
• Use longer phrases and give explanations.

8 A ▶ 8.14 Read the Skill box. Listen to six conversations and check (✓) the response that sounds more polite: a or b.

1 Tom, could you help me with this box? It's really heavy.   a ☐   b ☐
2 Do you feel like going to the movies tonight?   a ☐   b ☐
3 So what did your boss think of the designs?   a ☐   b ☐
4 Would you like to go for coffee after class?   a ☐   b ☐
5 Wow! That new jacket looks great on you.   a ☐   b ☐
6 Would you be interested in seeing my band play tomorrow evening? a ☐   b ☐

B ▶ 8.15 Listen and repeat the polite responses. Explain why they are more polite.

Go to Communication practice: Student A, page 163; Student B, page 171

9 A PREPARE In pairs, look at the diagram and discuss what you could say at each stage. You can make notes.

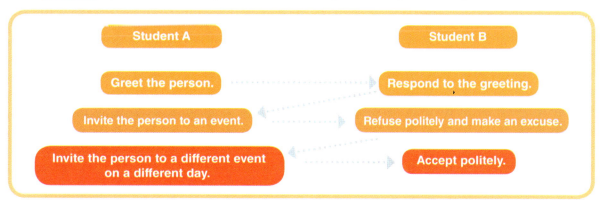

B PRACTICE Repeat your conversation until you can say it without looking at the diagram or your notes.

C PERSONAL BEST Work with another pair. Listen to their conversation. Did they use the same language as you? Was their conversation polite? In what way?

Personal Best Write another dialogue using the diagram in exercise 9A, but use different phrases.

73

7 and 8 REVIEW and PRACTICE

Grammar

1 Put a (X) by the sentence that is NOT correct.

1. a I haven't called Claude yet.
   b I've called Claude 10 minutes ago.
   c I called Claude 10 minutes ago.
2. a I have to wear a suit to work.
   b I can wear a suit to work.
   c I haven't to wear jeans to work.
3. a I've worked here since January.
   b I've worked here for five months.
   c I've worked here since five months ago.
4. a This restaurant is too crowded.
   b This restaurant isn't quiet enough.
   c This restaurant is too much crowded.
5. a I've seen the movie yet.
   b I saw the movie last week.
   c I've already seen the movie.
6. a You have too many clothes in your closet.
   b You can't have space enough for your clothes.
   c You don't have enough space in your closet.
7. a I haven't seen my parents for a month.
   b I didn't see my parents since last month.
   c I haven't seen my parents since last month.
8. a You can't walk on the grass.
   b You have to walk on the path.
   c You allowed to walk on the path.

2 Use the words in parentheses to write sentences that mean the same as the first sentence.

1. It's not necessary for Sofia to take the train.
   Sofia _____ take the train. (have)
2. I didn't have breakfast this morning.
   I _____ breakfast _____ today. (yet)
3. I went to the grocery store this morning.
   I _____ to the grocery store. (already)
4. We've had the car since March.
   We _____ six months. (for)
5. We need more bread.
   We _____ bread. (enough)
6. She hasn't visited me for years.
   She _____ 2012. (visited)
7. The coffee has more milk than I wanted.
   There's _____ in my coffee. (too)
8. You're not allowed to use your phone in here.
   You _____ your phone in here. (use)

3 Choose the correct options to complete the text.

Don't look down!

The city of Dubai [1]*built / has built* over 200 skyscrapers [2]*for / since* 2000, and the Burj Khalifa is the tallest of these. It's 830 m. high, with 163 floors and has an incredible 24,000 windows … all of which [3]*have / have to* be cleaned! The tallest part of the building is [4]*too / too much* difficult for people to clean, and machines are used. However, a team of 36 men clean the rest of the building. Let's talk to Bibek Thapa from Nepal, who has [5]*already / yet* finished cleaning for the day.

What's the hardest part about the job?
I've climbed [6]*enough mountains / mountains enough* in Nepal not to be afraid of heights. The worst thing for me is the sun. Sometimes it's [7]*too / too much* hot, and we [8]*have to / can't* wear protective clothing.

What's it like in bad weather?
We don't work when there's [9]*too many / too much* wind or dust because it's very dangerous.

Do you need any special equipment?
We use lots of safety equipment, obviously, but we [10]*have to / don't have to* use any special cleaning chemicals. We just use soap and water, like when you clean windows at home.

Vocabulary

1 Match the words with the definitions.

> rush hour   fresh   start out   coconut
> raw   crosswalk   turkey
> give someone a ride   trash can   commuter

1. to take someone to a place in your car _____
2. a place for garbage when you're on the street _____
3. a person who travels to work _____
4. a large bird we can eat _____
5. a large fruit from a palm tree _____
6. to leave your house to go somewhere _____
7. food that is not cooked _____
8. a place where you can cross the street safely _____
9. the busiest time of day on the street _____
10. food that was prepared recently _____

REVIEW and PRACTICE 7 and 8

2 Circle the word that is different. Explain your answer.

1	passenger	platform	pedestrian	commuter
2	sour	sweet	bitter	crunchy
3	drive	ride	go by	traffic
4	beef	lamb	shrimp	turkey
5	tunnel	bridge	bike lane	trash can
6	delayed	street sign	statue	sidewalk
7	tuna	peach	pineapple	strawberry
8	tasty	burned	healthy	delicious

3 Choose the correct word to complete the sentences.

1 My bus never _____ on time.
 a arrives   b gets   c drives
2 Is the fish _____? It doesn't smell very good.
 a fresh   b tasty   c healthy
3 We _____ early on our hike at 9:00.
 a arrive   b started out   c drive
4 We're having _____ for dessert.
 a flour   b lettuce   c apple pie
5 My car is at the garage, so I can't _____ to work.
 a ride   b drive   c arrive
6 A: What's on the pizza?
 B: There's tomato sauce, peppers, and _____ .
 a flour   b cheese   c cereal
7 There are no _____ on this street; it's very dark!
 a traffic lights   b streetlights   c street signs
8 The doctor said I shouldn't eat _____ food.
 a fresh   b salty   c disgusting

4 Complete the conversations with the words in the boxes.

parking space   benches   parking lot
apartment building   public transportation

Jo   Is your new ¹_____ near the city bridge?
Lee   No, it's next to the square with the fountain and all the ²_____ to sit on.
Jo   That's a great area! Do you get a ³_____ for your car?
Lee   Yes, but I use ⁴_____ to get to work because my office doesn't have a ⁵_____ .

fresh   delicious   seafood   spicy   vegetarian

Kim   Don't forget you have to cook ⁶_____ food for my parents. They don't eat meat.
Jon   I know. I'm going to cook curry.
Kim   Don't cook curry! It will be too ⁷_____ for them! Why don't you cook the *paella* you made last week? It was ⁸_____ ! I loved it.
Jon   But that had ⁹_____ in it!
Kim   Oh, yeah. Can't you make it without it? Just add lots of ¹⁰_____ vegetables.

75

UNIT 9
Money and shopping

LANGUAGE | used to ■ money verbs

9A He used to be poor

1 A Look at the title of the text and the pictures. Discuss the questions in pairs.
1. Have you ever been to a Zara store?
2. What does Zara sell?
3. Who is the man?
4. What does the title of the text mean?

B Read the introduction and check your answers.

FROM ZERO TO ZARA

Today, he's one of the richest men in the world with a global business that is worth billions of dollars, but he used to be a poor boy from Galicia, in the north of Spain. This is the story of Amancio Ortega, the founder of the clothing company, Zara.

Amancio was born in 1936. His father was a railway worker and didn't earn much money. The family sometimes couldn't afford food. His mother used to ask for credit at the grocery store, but one day they said no. At that moment, Amancio decided to quit school and get a job. He was just 14.

Amancio's first job was at a shirt store. He used to fold the shirts and deliver them to customers on his bike. Then he moved to another store, where he learned a lot about the industry. Clothes used to be very expensive, and there wasn't much to choose from, so customers didn't use to buy many. Amancio realized that if he could produce more attractive clothes more cheaply, people would spend more money.

So, at the age of 27, and with just a little money that he'd saved, Amancio started his own business making pajamas, which he sold to local stores. After borrowing some money from the bank, he began making other types of clothing, and the business grew. In 1975, Amancio opened his first Zara store, and the company soon opened more stores in Spain.

Today, you can find Zara and the other fashion companies Amancio owns in 88 different countries around the world, but he still lives in Galicia, where he grew up.

2 Order the events from 1–8. Read the text and check.
a ☐ He worked in a shirt store.
b ☐ Zara expanded around the world.
c ☐ He quit school.
d ☐ The first Zara store opened.
e ☐ He started to produce other types of clothing.
f ☐ Amancio was born in northern Spain.
g ☐ He used his own money to start a business.
h ☐ He asked the bank for some money.

3 What do you think Amancio Ortega is like? Why?

4 A Match the two columns to make sentences. Check your answers in the text.
1. Amancio decided to
2. His mother used to
3. Customers didn't use to
4. He used to

a ask for credit.
b buy many clothes.
c quit school.
d be a poor boy from Galicia.

B Look at sentences 1–4 again and answer the questions. Then read the Grammar box.
1. Are the sentences about the past, the present, or the future? _____
2. Which sentence is an action that only happened once? ____ Which tense is it? _____
3. Which sentence is a situation that was true in the past, but isn't true now? ____
4. Which sentences are actions that happened more than once in the past? ____ ____

76

used to ■ money verbs **LANGUAGE 9A**

Grammar *used to*

Actions that happened regularly in the past, but don't happen now:
How **did** you **use to get** to school?
We **used to walk** to school. We **didn't use to take** the bus.

Situations that were true in the past, but aren't true now:
What **did** she **use to be** like?
She **used to be** really shy. She **didn't use to be** very confident.

Look! We use the simple past for an action that only happened once.
I **went** shopping yesterday. NOT ~~I used to go shopping yesterday~~.

Go to Grammar practice: *used to*, page 128

5 ▶ 9.2 **Pronunciation:** *used to/use to* Listen to the sentences. How do you say the words in **bold**? Do they sound different? Listen again and repeat.
1 His family **used to** be poor.
2 He didn't **use to** earn much money.
3 Did he **use to** work from home?

Go to Communication practice: Student A, page 163; Student B, page 171

6 Match the words in the box with definitions 1–6. Look at the highlighted words in the text on page 76 to help you.

be worth   earn   can afford   spend   save   borrow

1 have enough money to buy something _____
2 not use money and keep it in a bank _____
3 use money to buy something _____
4 have a value of a certain amount of money _____
5 take money from someone, but return it later _____
6 make money from work _____

Go to Vocabulary practice: money verbs, page 151

7 Discuss the questions in pairs.
1 What do you spend your money on?
2 Do you find it difficult to save money?
3 Do you own your home or do you rent it?
4 Which professions earn the most money?
5 Have you ever borrowed money from a bank?
6 Do you have a car? How much is it worth?
7 Do you think athletes get paid too much money?
8 Do you ever waste money on things you don't need?

8 A ▶ 9.4 Listen to five people talking about their childhood. Match the topics in the box with the speakers.

bedtime   money   toys   vacations   food

1 Rachel _____   2 Allan _____   3 Freddy _____   4 Lucy _____   5 Sam _____

B ▶ 9.4 Complete the sentences with the simple past or *used to* form of the verbs in parentheses. Listen again and check.
1 The first book I _____ was *Northern Lights*. (buy)
2 Our parents _____ about us. (not worry)
3 We _____ for dinner every Saturday night. (go out)
4 My grandpa always _____ me a story in bed at night. (read)
5 I _____ a Buzz Lightyear toy for my birthday one year. (get)

9 A In pairs, talk about your childhood. Use the topics in the boxes or your own ideas.

I used to go to bed at 7:00 p.m. every night. What time did you use to go to bed?

B Tell the class some things that you found out about your partner.
He/She used to …   He/She didn't use to …

Personal Best Write ten sentences about you, using the verbs from the Vocabulary practice.

77

9 SKILLS LISTENING identifying attitude and opinion ■ filler expressions ■ shopping

9B What a bargain!

1 Match the options in the box with pictures a–f.

> discount   cash register   shopping center/mall   cash   line   receipt

Go to Vocabulary practice: shopping, page 151

2 Discuss the questions in pairs.
1 Do you prefer to shop in malls, department stores, small independent stores, or online? Why?
2 Have you ever found a bargain during a sale? If so, what was it?
3 Do you always try on clothes in the dressing rooms before buying them? Why/Why not?
4 How long do you keep a receipt after you have bought something? Why?
5 Do you ever go window shopping? Why/Why not?

3 ▶ 9.7   Watch or listen to the first part of *Learning Curve*. Check (✓) the best summary of what Ethan says.
a Shopping in the past was very different. ☐
b Shopping centers have a long history. ☐
c Shopping centers or malls are the best place to find bargains. ☐

4 ▶ 9.7   What do sentences 1–6 refer to: *Trajan's Market* (TM), or *Grand Bazaar* (GB)? Watch or listen again and check.

1 It is about 600 years old.   ____
2 Today it's a museum.   ____
3 It has about 5,000 stores.   ____
4 It has about 250,000 visitors per day.   ____
5 It's almost 2,000 years old.   ____
6 People used to live there.   ____

5 A Check (✓) Kate's opinion of the Grand Bazaar.
a She thinks it's an interesting place for tourists. ☐
b She thinks it's a good place to go shopping. ☐
c She prefers modern shopping malls. ☐

B Can you remember what words she used to give this opinion? Read the Skill box.

Ethan

identifying attitude and opinion ■ filler expressions ■ shopping   **LISTENING**   SKILLS **9B**

Skill   identifying attitude and opinion

It's often important to understand what someone's personal opinion is.
- Listen for phrases that we use to give opinions: *I think ..., I'd say ..., to be honest ...,* etc.
- Listen for adjectives that describe feelings: *boring, excited, upset, annoyed, pleased,* etc.
- Listen for verbs that express attitude: *look forward to, prefer, love, have to,* etc.

6 ▶ 9.8 Watch or listen to the second part of the show. Match the reasons for going to a shopping center in the box with the three people.

see a movie   return something to a store   meet up with friends

Andrea

Lohi

Joan

7 A ▶ 9.8 Watch or listen again. Are the sentences true (T) or false (F)?
1 Andrea is annoyed that her friends aren't coming.   ____
2 She doesn't like "queues" (lines).   ____
3 Lohi is surprised at the size of the mall.   ____
4 He thinks he made a mistake shopping there.   ____
5 Joan was angry because she couldn't exchange her jumper.   ____
6 She's happy with her new jumper.   ____

B Can you remember the words and phrases that helped you answer the questions?

8 Discuss the questions in pairs.
1 When did you last go to a shopping center?
2 Did you buy anything? If so, how did you pay?
3 What were the last clothes you bought?
4 Did you try them on?

9 ▶ 9.9 Read what Andrea said. Can you understand it without the missing words? Listen and complete the sentences.

> 1_____ , I'm supposed to be meeting up with some friends, but 2_____ , they 3_____ , just texted me to say they're not coming. I'd say it's a bit rude really, but I can't do anything. So, I'm just 4_____ of looking around, window shopping, 5_____ ?

Listening builder   filler expressions

Fillers are words and phrases that speakers say to give themselves time to think. They don't really mean anything:
So, I bought this jacket, *like*, a week ago, *I mean*, I wanted to *kind of* return it and, *er*, get a refund.
Well, I don't have the receipt, *you see*, because I *I guess* lost it.

10 ▶ 9.10 Read the Listening builder. Listen to the conversation and answer the questions.
1 What is Jason doing at the shopping center?
2 Which filler expressions do you hear?

11 In pairs, discuss how shopping has changed from the past. Use the topics in the boxes or your own ideas.

size of stores   opening hours   location   customer service   choice   quality of products   ways to pay   prices

I think the quality of clothes used to be much better.

Personal Best Use your ideas from exercise 11 to write a paragraph about how shopping has changed.

9 LANGUAGE the passive

9C Going, going, gone!

1 Ask and answer the questions in pairs.
1 Have you ever been to an auction? Where was it?
2 Have you ever bought anything on an online auction website?
3 What did you buy? How much did you pay?

2 ▶ 9.11 Look at the pictures. In pairs, match four of the prices in the box with the items that were sold at auctions. Listen and check.

$5,000 $100,000 $1.8M $4.6M $75M $120M

a

b

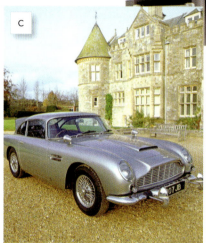
c

d

3 ▶ 9.11 In pairs, try to complete the sentences. Listen again and check.
1 *The Scream* **was painted** in _____ by Edvard Munch.
2 This version **is thought** to be _____ by many experts.
3 The jacket **was worn by** Michael Jackson in the music video for _____ .
4 It's **made** of red and black _____ .
5 The Aston Martin car **was driven by** Sean Connery in the _____ movies.
6 Another car from the movies **was stolen** in _____ .
7 Vegemite **is eaten by** millions of _____ every day.
8 This piece of toast **was given** to Niall Horan from _____ on an Australian TV show.

4 Look at the words in **bold** in exercise 3. Answer the questions. Then read the Grammar box.
1 Which grammar structure is used in the sentences? _____
2 Which sentences are in the simple present? _____ Which are in the simple past? _____
3 How do we make this structure? The verb _____ + the _____ of the main verb.
4 Which word do we use before the people who do/did the action? _____
5 What is more important in the passive: the people who do/did the action or the action? _____

Grammar the passive

Simple present passive
Where **are** the cars **made**?
They **are made** in Italy.
They **aren't made** anywhere else.

Simple past passive
When **was** the book **written**?
It **was written** in 1957.
It **wasn't published** until 2015.

Look! To say who does/did the action we use ***by***.
The cars are made **by factory workers**.   The book was written **by Harper Lee**.

Go to Grammar practice: the passive, page 129

the passive LANGUAGE 9C

5 A ▶ 9.13 **Pronunciation: sentence stress** Listen and repeat the sentence. Pay attention to the underlined stressed words.

The <u>picture</u> was <u>painted</u> in <u>1945</u>.

B ▶ 9.14 Underline the stressed words. Listen, check, and repeat.
1 These clothes were worn by Lady Gaga.
2 These peaches are grown in Brazil.
3 The salmon is cooked with lemon.
4 The car was driven by Lewis Hamilton.
5 These watches are made in Switzerland.
6 The bridge was opened in 2010.

Go to Communication practice: Student A, page 163; Student B, page 171

6 Look at the picture and the title. What do you think the text is about? How much is the box worth? Read the text and check.

FAMILY FINDS "LOST" TREASURE IN FATHER'S HOME

This beautiful wood and gold box was made in Japan in 1640. It is one of ten boxes that were made in Kyoto by Kaomi Nagashige, a well-known Japanese artist. However, this box was thought to be lost. In fact, the Victoria and Albert Museum in London had spent over fifty years searching for it. Unknown to the museum, the box was just one kilometer away in a nearby house. It was bought by a French engineer for £100 in 1970, and amazingly, it was used as a table for his television! After he died, his family decided to sell it, and it was identified by art experts as one of the lost Japanese boxes from 1640. It went up for auction, and was sold to the Rijksmuseum in Amsterdam for 7.3 million euros, making the family millionaires.

7 A Use the words to make passive questions.
1 what / the box / make of ?
   _____
2 where / the box / make ?
   _____
3 when / the box / make ?
   _____
4 who / the box / buy / by / in 1970 ?
   _____
5 how much / the box / buy / for ?
   _____
6 what / the box / use / for ?
   _____
7 who / the box / identify / by ?
   _____
8 who / the box / sell / to / for 7.3 million euros?
   _____

B Ask and answer the questions in pairs.

8 Discuss the questions in pairs.
1 Do you think the box is really worth so much money?
2 How would you feel if you were the family of the French engineer?
3 What is your most important possession? Would you ever sell it?

9 Answer the quiz questions in pairs.

Quiz Time
① Where are roubles used as money?
② Who was *The Alchemist* written by?
③ When was penicillin discovered?
④ Which U.S. city is known as "The Big Apple"?
⑤ How many Harry Potter movies were made?
⑥ Which languages are spoken in Canada?

10 A In pairs, write five quiz questions with the passive form of the verbs in the boxes.

| invent | make | sing | direct | wear | write | paint | record | know | discover | use | win |

B Exchange quizzes with another pair and answer the questions.

Personal Best Write about an important possession and say how much it is worth to you.

9 SKILLS WRITING writing a formal e-mail ■ noun forms of verbs

9D I'd like a refund!

1 What are the advantages and disadvantages of online shopping? Discuss the questions in pairs.

1. How often do you buy things online?
2. What do you prefer to buy in stores? Why?
3. Have you ever had a problem with something you bought online?

2 Match the problems in the box with pictures a–e.

> The wrong size was sent.   It was broken or damaged.   Part of the order was missing.
> The order arrived late / didn't arrive.   I was charged too much.

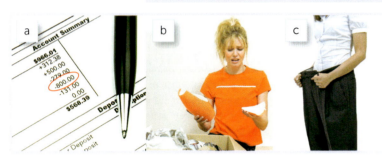

3 Read the e-mail and answer the questions.

1. What are the three problems with Valerie's order?
2. What did she pay extra for?
3. What does she want the company to do?
4. Would you use this company?

To: info@phonetastic.com
Subject: Problems with my order (P389746-D)

Dear Sir/Madam:
I am writing to complain about the problems I have had with my online order (P389746-D).
I ordered a red X3 smartphone from your website on January 14, and I paid $4.99 extra for next-day delivery. I waited for one week, but nothing arrived, so I contacted your customer service team. I was told that it was on its way. However, the phone was only delivered yesterday—two weeks after I ordered it. Apart from the late delivery, there are two other problems with the phone. First, it is the wrong color. The phone I was sent is black, not red. And second, the screen is cracked. I have attached a photo so you can see what I mean. Because of these problems, I wish to return the phone and I would like a full refund, including the extra delivery charge.
I look forward to hearing from you soon.
Regards,
Valerie Lemoir

4 A Is the style of the e-mail formal or informal? Why?

B Order the different parts of the e-mail. Then read the Skill box.

a ☐ say what she wants the company to do
b ☐ complain about the late delivery
c ☐ give the reason for writing
d ☐ end the e-mail
e ☐ explain the other problems
f ☐ include a short and accurate subject line

 Skill writing a formal e-mail

We often write formal e-mails to people who work for other companies and organizations.
- Use a formal greeting: *Dear Sir/Madam: Dear Mrs. Jones:*
- Order your paragraphs: reason for writing, explaining the situation, what you want to happen
- Avoid contractions: *I am writing* ... NOT ~~I'm writing~~ ...
- Use formal expressions: *I contacted* ... NOT ~~I called~~ ...
- Use passives to avoid being personal: *I was told* ... NOT ~~They told me~~ ...

writing a formal e-mail ■ noun forms of verbs   WRITING   SKILLS   9D

5 Choose the correct options to complete the reply from Suleiman.

To: valerie.lemoir@mailshop.com
Subject: RE: Problems with my order (P389746-D)

¹*Hi Valerie. / Dear Ms. Lemoir:*
I am writing ²*in regard to / about* your e-mail of January 29.
First, ³*I feel bad about / please accept my apologies for* the problems you experienced with our online ordering system, which were ⁴*unacceptable / really bad*. Unfortunately, ⁵*the wrong software was installed / they installed the wrong software* and this has caused some unexpected problems.
Therefore, I ⁶*would be very happy to refund / don't mind refunding* the money, including all delivery costs that ⁷*you were charged / they charged*. Please ⁸*tell me / advise me of* a convenient date for our delivery team to pick up the phone. ⁹*In addition to this / Also*, I would like to offer you a $50 gift certificate to spend on any product at Phonetastic. I hope this is satisfactory, and we look forward to you shopping with us in future.
¹⁰*Cheers! / Sincerely* yours,

Suleiman Malik
Customer Services Manager

6 How did Suleiman try to solve the problem? Do you think Valerie will use the company again?

7 A Complete the sentences from Valerie's e-mail with the words in the box. Check your answers in her e-mail.

delivered   delivery   order   ordered

1 I am writing to complain about the problems I have had with my online _____ ...
2 I _____ a red X3 smartphone from your website on ...
3 However, the phone was only _____ yesterday–two weeks after I ordered it.
4 Apart from the late _____ , there are ...

B How does Valerie repeat her ideas without repeating the exact words?

| Text builder | noun forms of verbs |

No change:	order → order	**Noun ends in -sion:**	decide → decision
Noun ends in -ment:	argue → argument	**Noun ends in -ation:**	inform → information
Noun ends in -y:	deliver → delivery		

8 Read the Text builder. Complete the sentences with the noun form of the verbs in parentheses.
1 There's a problem with the _____ on this credit card. (pay)
2 We have received your _____ for the job. (apply)
3 In _____, this is a serious problem. (conclude)
4 I didn't receive an _____ for their mistakes. (apologize)
5 He hasn't given me an _____ yet. (answer)

9 A PREPARE Choose a problem with an online order. Make notes about the details of the problem and what you want the company to do (e.g., contact you/exchange/refund).

missing part   arrived 3 days late

wrong color

wrong product delivered

B PRACTICE Use the Skill box to write a formal e-mail complaining about the order. Repeat your ideas in different ways using noun and verb forms of words.

C PERSONAL BEST Exchange e-mails with your partner. Check (✓) three sentences you think are very good. Suggest three ways to improve his/her e-mail.

Personal Best   Write the company's reply to your partner's e-mail from exercise 9.

UNIT 10 Sports and fitness

LANGUAGE past perfect ■ sports and competitions

10A Winning is everything!

1 ▶ 10.1 Listen and match the speakers with pictures a–c.

2 ▶ 10.1 Complete the sentences with the words in the box. Listen again and check.

> beat   win   game   race   umpire   athlete   medal   trophy   score   crowd

1 The _____ is almost over. In one minute, Real Madrid will _____ the game and the _____. But wait. What's this? Here comes Arsenal. The ball goes to Walcott. He has to _____ a goal, now. He does!
2 Serena Williams to serve. Was that out? She looks at the _____. You can hear the _____ cheering. They're sure Serena is going to _____ her sister, Venus.
3 Here they come, the finish line of the 100-meter _____, and Bolt is going to win the gold _____ again. Yes, he's done it. What an amazing _____!

Go to Vocabulary practice: sports and competitions, page 152

3 Discuss the questions in pairs.

1 Do you prefer to watch or take part in sports?
2 Have you ever won a medal or a trophy?
3 Would you like to be a professional athlete?
4 How have sports changed over the last 100 years?

4 Read the text. What are the names of the athletes in the pictures?

THE TOUGHEST RACE EVER?

There are some difficult events in the Olympic Games, but nothing compares with the 1904 Olympic Marathon. One athlete almost died, and the race ended in a public scandal.

The marathon started on an incredibly hot day in St. Louis, in the U.S., and there were lots of cars and horses on the dusty roads. One athlete, William Garcia, started coughing after he'd breathed in too much dust. It was so bad he had to quit the race and was taken to the hospital. Another runner, Len Tau from South Africa, eventually finished in ninth place, but he was disappointed because some wild dogs had chased him for over a mile in the opposite direction during the race!

Meanwhile, the first athlete to cross the finish line was an American, Fred Lorz. The crowd thought a local athlete had won, so they started celebrating, but actually, Lorz had cheated. He'd started feeling sick during the race and had ridden 11 miles in a car! Fortunately, a spectator had seen Lorz getting out of the car one mile before the finish line and told the referee, so Lorz didn't win the gold medal.

The next runner to finish was another American, Tom Hicks. Hicks hadn't felt well either, so his friends had given him a drink of eggs mixed with some chemicals to help him. However, this had made him feel even worse and, in the end, his friends had helped him walk the final part of the race. Even though he hadn't run the whole marathon on his own, the organizers presented Hicks with the gold medal after the hardest marathon of all time.

84

past perfect ■ sports and competitions   **LANGUAGE 10A**

5 A Read the sentences. Check (✓) the action that happened first: **a** or **b**?

1 a ☐ William Garcia **started** coughing after   b ☐ he**'d breathed** in too much dust.
2 a ☐ Len Tau **was** disappointed because   b ☐ some wild dogs **had chased** him for over a mile.
3 a ☐ The crowd thought a local athlete **had won**, so b ☐ they **started** celebrating.
4 a ☐ Even though he **hadn't run** the whole marathon, b ☐ the organizers **presented** Hicks with the gold medal.

B Look at the verbs in **bold** in exercise 5A and answer the questions. Then read the Grammar box.

1 What tense are the actions that happened first? *simple past / past perfect*
2 What tense are the actions that happened later? *simple past / past perfect*
3 How do we form the past perfect? _____ + _____

Grammar past perfect

An action that happened before another action in the past:
I **had forgotten** my keys, so I couldn't open the door.   I explained to my boss that I **hadn't finished** the report.
Had you **eaten** anything before you went swimming?   When I got to the party, my friend **had gone** home.

Go to Grammar practice: past perfect, page 130

6 ▶10.6 **Pronunciation:** *'d /hadn't* Listen to the sentences. How do you say *'d* and *hadn't*? Listen again and repeat.

1 He**'d** breathed in too much dust.   2 He **hadn't** run the whole marathon by himself.

7 A Complete the sentences with the past perfect form of the verbs in parentheses.

1 They _____ before the game. (not warm up)   3 She _____ a rugby game before. (not see)
2 I knew they _____! (cheat)   4 We celebrated because he _____ a goal. (score)

B ▶10.7 In pairs, say the sentences. Pay attention to the *'d/hadn't* contractions. Listen, check, and repeat.

Go to Communication practice: Student A, page 164; Student B, page 172

8 ▶10.8 Complete the text with the correct form of the verbs in parentheses. Use the simple past or past perfect. Listen and check.

There are eleven players on a soccer team, but in this team photo of Manchester United there are twelve–so who's the twelfth man? The team [1]_____ (be) very excited after they [2]_____ (travel) to Germany for their Champions League game against Bayern Munich. The players [3]_____ (line up) for a photo when suddenly Karl Power [4]_____ (run) onto the playing field dressed in the Manchester United uniform and [5]_____ (stand) next to them. Even though some of the players [6]_____ (notice) Karl, the photographer still [7]_____ (take) the photo. Karl then [8]_____ (go) back to his seat to watch the game. Unfortunately, Manchester United [9]_____ (lose), but Karl was happy because he [10]_____ (meet) his heroes!

9 A In pairs, write as many sentences as you can about the pictures. Use the simple past and past perfect.

He was very disappointed because he'd lost the game.

a

b

c

B Tell the class your most interesting sentence. Who has the most original explanation?

Personal Best Write about an occasion when you did something that you had never done before.

85

10 SKILLS READING finding information in a text ■ giving examples

10B Rock 'n' roll on wheels

1 Look at the pictures and the title of the text on page 87. Answer the questions.

1 What are the Paralympic Games?
2 Have you ever seen a wheelchair rugby game?
3 Would you like to take part in a game?
4 What kind of person do you think Laura is?

Skill finding information in a text

When we want to find information in a longer text, we need to know where to look.
- Read the text quickly and understand the general topic of each paragraph.
- Read the question carefully and underline any key words.
- Match the question with the paragraph that has the information you need.
- Read this paragraph in detail to answer the question.

2 Read the Skill box. Then read the text quickly and match paragraphs A–G with topics 1–7.

1 how it feels to play wheelchair rugby ____
2 how to find out more about the sport ____
3 creating interest in disabled sports ____
4 Laura's physical appearance ____
5 media interest in wheelchair rugby ____
6 the origins of the sport ____
7 the rules of wheelchair rugby ____

3 **A** Read the questions. Underline the key words and match them with paragraphs A–G.

	Paragraph	Answer
1 How long does it take Tim to cross the court?	____	_____
2 Which movie did wheelchair rugby appear in?	____	_____
3 What other wheelchair sports are there?	____	_____
4 When was wheelchair rugby invented?	____	_____
5 What is the official wheelchair rugby organization?	____	_____
6 Where does Laura have a bandage?	____	_____
7 How many players are on a wheelchair rugby team?	____	_____

B Read the paragraphs and answer the questions.

4 Did you know anything about wheelchair rugby before you read the article? Would you like to watch a game?

5 Find the highlighted words in the text.

1 Which words come before nouns?
2 Which words come at the start of a sentence?

Text builder giving examples

Listing examples:
*I'd like to visit countries in south-east Asia, **like** Thailand and Vietnam.*
*You shouldn't eat unhealthy food, **such as** pizzas or hamburgers.*

Giving an example phrase:
*She's had problems at work. **For example,** she arrived late every day last week.*

Look! We can also use **for instance** instead of *for example* with no change in meaning:
*She's had problems at work. **For instance**, she arrived late every day last week.*

6 Read the Text builder. Complete the sentences with your own ideas. Compare your sentences in pairs.

1 Cheating has become very common in some sports. For example, …
2 My country has produced some famous athletes, like …
3 Some sports can be very dangerous, such as …

7 **A** In pairs, choose an interesting sport. Prepare a short talk about it. Use the ideas in the boxes.

where it is played the rules how popular it is famous players how it feels to play media interest

B Tell another pair about your sport. Would you like to try this sport?

86

finding information in a text ■ giving examples   READING   SKILLS   10B

Sports interview:
Tim White meets wheelchair rugby player, Laura Sabetta

A
The first thing I notice about Laura Sabetta is her arms. They're almost as big as my legs. The next thing I notice is a bandage on her arm. "I get injuries fairly often because we play to win," the Argentinian athlete explains,"… it's rugby, after all."

B
Wheelchair rugby has always been a tough, physical sport. Invented in Canada in 1977, it was first called "murderball." As the sport's popularity grew, the name changed to the more serious "wheelchair rugby." It was a new name, but the game was just as violent.

C
People who have never played the sport might think of it as a fun way to spend an afternoon, but it's exhausting. Laura gives me a special wheelchair, and I move slowly onto the court. I wear gloves, but it's very hard work pushing the chair using only my arms. Wheelchair rugby is played on a basketball court that measures 28 x 15 meters, and it takes me over three minutes to cross it. Meanwhile, Laura has already finished warming up.

D
I'm soon happy to join the spectators and watch the game. Wheelchair rugby is a mix of basketball, rugby, and hockey. Two teams of four players throw and carry a volleyball, trying to score goals. Players score when their wheels cross the line at the end of the court while they are holding the ball in their hands.

E
Wheelchair rugby's popularity exploded after it featured in the 2005 movie *Murderball*. Many of its players are now big names in Paralympic sports, like the star of the movie, Mark Zupan. The sport is now played in more than 25 countries, such as Japan and the U.S. So, however you look at it, wheelchair rugby is big news.

F
This places lots of responsibility on the players, as Laura explains. "There are lots of sports opportunities out there for people who need a wheelchair, such as skiing, tennis, and sailing. The important thing is making sure people know about them, so they can take part. We also need fans. We want big crowds watching the game. That's why I'm doing this interview!"

G
Getting involved is easy. There's plenty of information online. For example, there's the website of the International Wheelchair Rugby Federation at www.iwrf.com. It's also fairly easy to find a game in most large towns if you just want to watch. Many people only watch the sport once every four years at the Paralympic Games, but as Laura tells me, "For people like me, this isn't a hobby. Since I lost the use of my legs, it's been my life."

Personal Best — Write five more questions about the wheelchair rugby interview.

87

10 LANGUAGE   reported speech ■ parts of the body

10C He said it had changed his life

1 Match the words in the box with the parts of the body.

chest   knee   shoulder   elbow   neck   wrist

1 _____   3 _____   5 _____
2 _____   4 _____   6 _____

Go to Vocabulary practice: parts of the body, page 153

2 A Look at the poster. Discuss the questions in pairs.
1 How much exercise do doctors recommend you get each week?
2 Is it possible to get in shape with three minutes of exercise a week?
3 What do you think "high-intensity interval training (HIIT)" is?

B ▶10.10   Listen to an interview and check your answers.

3 Discuss the questions in pairs.
1 How much exercise do you get a week? What do you do?
2 Do you believe that high-intensity training works? Why/Why not?
3 Would you like to try high-intensity training? Why/Why not?

4 A ▶10.10   Complete the sentences about what Carlos and Vicky said. Listen again and check.
1 Carlos said that in HIIT you used almost all your _____.
2 Carlos said two years ago he had weighed almost _____ kg.
3 Carlos said he was eating more _____ and _____ now.
4 Carlos said that he had lost _____ kg.
5 Carlos told Vicky that first she would do some gentle cycling to _____.
6 Vicky told Carlos she was going to try _____ seconds of high-intensity cycling.

B Look at the sentences 1–6 again and answer the questions.
1 Which two verbs do we use to report what someone says in the past? _____ _____
2 Which verb do we use when we say who the person is talking to? _____
3 Is it always necessary to use *that* with these verbs? Yes / No

5 A ▶10.11   Listen carefully to what Carlos and Vicky said. Write the verbs they used.

1 In HIIT, you _____ almost all your muscles.
2 Well, two years ago I _____ almost 100 kg.
3 Oh, and I _____ more fruit and vegetables now.
4 Of course–75 kg. I _____ 25 kg.
5 OK, so first you _____ some gentle cycling to warm up.
6 Thanks, Carlos. Well, I _____ 20 seconds of high-intensity cycling now.

B Compare the verbs in exercise 5A with the verbs in exercise 4A. How have they changed? Then read the Grammar box.

1 simple present → *simple past*
2 simple past → _____
3 present continuous → _____
4 present perfect → _____
5 will → _____
6 am/are/is going to → _____

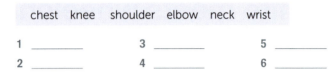

HIGH-INTENSITY TRAINING
GET IN SHAPE WITH THREE MINUTES OF EXERCISE PER WEEK

Personal Best

88

reported speech ■ parts of the body   **LANGUAGE 10C**

Grammar   reported speech

Direct speech:	Reported speech:
"*I play tennis.*"	She said (that) she **played** tennis.
"*Vicky tried HIIT.*"	He said (that) Vicky **had tried** HIIT.
"*It's raining.*"	They said (that) it **was raining**.
"*She hasn't arrived yet.*"	You said (that) she **hadn't arrived** yet.
"*I'll help you.*"	You said (that) you **would help** me.
"*We're going to call you.*"	They said (that) they **were going to call** me.
"*Ravi can't come to work.*"	She said (that) Ravi **couldn't come** to work.

Look! We use **told** to say who the person talked to: She **told me** (that) she played tennis.

Go to Grammar practice: reported speech, page 131

6 ▶ 10.13   Match the sentences in the box with the people. Listen and check.

> I go to the gym to meet my friends.   I'll tell my husband because he needs to lose weight.
> I can't do HIIT at my age!   I've tried it, but I hurt my shoulder.

Rosa   Kurt   Barry   Jessica

7 ▶ 10.14   **Pronunciation: weak form of *that*** Listen to the sentences. <u>Underline</u> the stressed words. How do we pronounce *that*? Listen again, check, and repeat.

1 Carlos said that HIIT was very popular.
2 He told me that I should ask some other people what they think.

8 A Complete the sentences using the information from exercise 6.

1 Rosa said that _____ .
2 Kurt told Vicky that _____ .
3 Barry told her that _____ .
4 Jessica said that _____ .

B ▶ 10.15   In pairs, practice saying sentences 1–4. Pay attention to the pronunciation of *that*. Listen, check, and repeat.

9 In pairs, ask and answer the question *What did … say?* Use reported speech to answer the questions.

A *What did José say?*   **B** *He said that he …*

1 I can't go running because I've hurt my ankle.
José

2 My bus is late, so I'm not going to be on time.
Sara

3 Our teacher is wearing a leather jacket.
Laura

4 If you're tired, I'll make you coffee.
David

Go to Communication practice: Student A, page 164; Student B, page 172

10 A In pairs, ask and answer the questions. Make notes of your partner's answers.

1 Have you ever run a long distance?
2 What was the first movie you saw at a movie theater?
3 What are you going to do this weekend?
4 Can you play any unusual sports?
5 What series are you watching on TV right now?
6 What are you doing after today's class?

B Work with another student. Report what your first partner said about questions 1–6.

Personal Best   Think of a news story or an interview with an athlete. Write what the person said.

89

SKILLS SPEAKING making inquiries ■ being helpful

10D Could you tell me …?

1 Discuss the questions in pairs.
1 What are the best ways to stay in shape?
2 Have you ever thought about joining a gym?
3 What would be important for you if you joined a gym?
4 Look at the web page. Would you join this gym? Why/Why not?

2 ▶ 10.16 Watch or listen to the first part of *Learning Curve*. Why does Marc want to join the gym?

3 ▶ 10.16 Watch or listen again and complete the web page with the correct information.

| OUR CENTERS | GYM FACILITIES | SWIMMING POOL | FITNESS CLASSES | MEMBERSHIP | SCHEDULE |

CITY FITNESS

June offer First month FREE

Join today or speak to one of our advisers   JOIN NOW   CONTACT US

Standard membership fee: ¹_____ per month (minimum 12-month contract)
Access to all facilities while the center is open.

Off-peak hours membership fee: ²_____ per month (no contract, pay as you go)
Access to facilities: Mon–Fri ³_____ and ⁴_____, on weekends closes at 2:00 p.m.
Additional $15 fee for access to swimming pool, sauna, and steam room.

Swimming-only membership fee: ⁵_____ per month
Access to the swimming pool only: Mon–Sun, 9:00 a.m.–5:00 p.m.

Opening hours: 6.00 a.m.–9.00 p.m.   Student discount available: 15%

4 ▶ 10.17 Match the two columns to complete Marc's inquiries. Listen and check.

1 Could I speak to someone   a the cost, please?
2 Could you tell   b information about that?
3 Could you give me some   c thing.
4 I'd also like to ask about   d off-peak membership.
5 Just one more   e about joining the gym?
6 So can I just double check   f me the cost?

Conversation builder — making inquiries

Starting inquiries politely:
Could I speak to someone about …?
Could you give me some information about …, please?
Excuse me, I was hoping you could help me.

Asking for additional information:
I'd also like to ask about …
I was told … Is that true?
Just one more thing. Do you …?
Can I double check? Do you …?

5 Read the Conversation builder. Choose three subjects in the boxes. In pairs, make inquiries about City Fitness. Use the information on the web page to answer.

 student discount   opening hours   swimming-only membership
        June offer   how to join

making inquiries ■ being helpful   SKILLS   10D

6 A ▶10.18 Watch or listen to the second part of the show. Does Marc decide to join the gym?

B ▶10.18 Are the sentences true (T) or false (F)? Watch or listen again and check.

1 Marc thought Taylor worked at a different center. ____
2 Taylor likes this center because it's small. ____
3 The receptionist told Marc about all the facilities. ____
4 Taylor offers Marc a free training session as a special offer. ____
5 Marc wants to start training slowly. ____

7 ▶10.19 Listen and repeat the receptionist and Taylor's phrases when you hear the beeps. How are they helpful to Marc?

Skill being helpful

There are different ways to be helpful in English, especially with colleagues and customers.
- Use friendly intonation to show you are happy to help.
- Make offers and suggestions: *Would you like me to …?   Shall I …?   I'll … if you want.*
- Check to make sure the person is satisfied: *Does that sound OK?   Is there anything else I can help you with?*

8 A Read the Skill box. Are phrases 1–6 answers to questions (A), offers and suggestions (O), or checking to make sure the customer is satisfied (C)?

1 The nearest one is on the corner of Sutton Street. ____
2 Do you have any other questions? ____
3 I think it costs about $20 to go downtown. ____
4 I'll just print out a map of the area for you. ____
5 Would you like me to write that down for you? ____
6 Is there anything else you'd like to know? ____

B ▶10.20 Listen and repeat phrases 1–6. Pay attention to the intonation.

Go to Communication practice: Student A, page 164; Student B, page 172

9 Discuss the questions in pairs.

1 Have you ever worked with customers or the public? What did you do?
2 What's the most difficult thing about working with customers or the public?
3 Have you ever had a bad experience with customer service? What happened?
4 Can you think of a good experience with customer service? What happened?

10 A PREPARE Choose one of the situations. Use the phrases and your own ideas to prepare questions.

Travel agent
Vacations in the U.S.
Best city to visit
Cost of flights

Pharmacist
Medicine for the flu
How often to take it
Other advice to feel better

Sports store salesperson
Running shoes
Best type for long distance
Colors and sizes

B PRACTICE In pairs, make inquiries using your questions. Your partner should try to answer your questions and be as helpful as possible.

C PERSONAL BEST Were you a satisfied customer? What could your partner do differently to be more helpful? Choose another situation and make more inquiries.

Personal Best Write down five questions you could ask in a restaurant.

9 and 10 — REVIEW and PRACTICE

Grammar

1 Put an (**X**) by the sentence that is NOT correct.

1 a I used to have a bike, but then I sold it. ☐
   b I had a bike, but then I sold it. ☐
   c I used to have a bike, but then I used to sell it. ☐

2 a Cervantes wrote *Don Quixote*. ☐
   b *Don Quixote* was written by Cervantes. ☐
   c Cervantes was written *Don Quixote*. ☐

3 a He'd gone home because he'd forgotten his wallet. ☐
   b He went home because he'd forgotten his wallet. ☐
   c He'd forgotten his wallet, so he went home. ☐

4 a Emma said, "I'll be on time." ☐
   b Emma told me she would be on time. ☐
   c Emma said me she would be on time. ☐

5 a She didn't used to get much exercise. ☐
   b She didn't get much exercise. ☐
   c She didn't use to get much exercise. ☐

6 a The radio was invented by Marconi. ☐
   b The radio is invented by Marconi. ☐
   c Marconi invented the radio. ☐

7 a He was late because he had missed the bus. ☐
   b He missed the bus, so he was late. ☐
   c He had been late so he had missed the bus. ☐

8 a Pete said he was seeing the movie before. ☐
   b Pete said he had seen the move before. ☐
   c Pete said, "I've seen the movie before." ☐

2 Use the words in parentheses to write sentences that mean the same as the first sentence.

1 Someone stole my car last week.
   My car _____ someone last week. (stolen)

2 Neil said, "I haven't been to Greece."
   Neil said that _____ to Greece. (been)

3 When I was young I played the piano.
   I _____ the piano. (used)

4 They make Vespas in Italy.
   Vespas _____ in Italy. (are)

5 We ate our soup. Then he brought the drinks.
   When he brought the drinks, we _____ our soup. (had)

6 Kelly said, "I don't need any help."
   Kelly _____ any help. (me)

7 I didn't take an umbrella and I got wet.
   I got wet because I _____ an umbrella. (took)

8 I wasn't a very shy child.
   When I was a child, I _____ very shy. (be)

3 Complete the text with the correct form of the verbs in parentheses.

HOW NOT TO LOSE YOUR PET

Fumie Takahashi, a 64-year-old woman from Japan, was very happy when the police ¹_____ (tell) her that they ²_____ (find) her pet parakeet, Piko Chan. But the amazing thing was that the bird ³_____ (tell) the police its own address!

Mrs. Takahashi ⁴_____ (use / have) another parakeet, but it escaped and flew away. So, when she bought Piko Chan, she taught it to repeat her street name and house number. Last Sunday, Piko Chan also escaped, when the door to its cage ⁵_____ (leave) open. It flew to a nearby hotel and, after a few hours, it ⁶_____ (take) to the police station by a guest.

The police ⁷_____ (say) that the bird ⁸_____ (be) silent for two days, and they hadn't known what to do with it. Eventually, however, Piko Chan surprised them all when it ⁹_____ (tell) them where it ¹⁰_____ (live).

If Piko Chan escapes again, it'll probably be found even more quickly. Its photo has appeared in newspapers all over Tokyo, and Mrs. Takahashi recently took the bird to a press conference, where it told journalists its address again.

Vocabulary

1 Put the words in the box in the correct columns.

| receipt cash register ankle crowd knee refund |
| medal sales referee cheek beat chin |

the body	sports	shopping

92

REVIEW and PRACTICE — 9 and 10

2 Complete the conversation with the correct words.

Lena These jeans look amazing! Where is the ¹d *ressing* r *oom* ?

Peter Over there, but can you ²a _____ to buy them? I didn't think you had much money right now.

Lena Probably not. I don't ³g _____ p _____ until the end of the month. Can I ⁴b _____ some money from you?

Peter You already ⁵o _____ me 50 dollars!

Lena I'll ⁶p _____ you b _____ all the money at the end of the month. I promise.

Peter OK, ⁷t _____ o _____ the jeans. If they ⁸f _____ you, I'll think about it.

Lena Thanks, Peter! There's a 70% ⁹d _____ on them today; they're a real ¹⁰b _____.

Peter OK, Lena.

3 Circle the word that is different. Explain your answer.

1	win	tie	lose	score
2	earn	borrow	lend	pay back
3	bargain	game	discount	a sale
4	return	exchange	deliver	refund
5	finger	thumb	chest	hand
6	medal	umpire	trophy	race
7	knee	elbow	shoulder	forehead
8	shopping center	department store	supermarket	dressing room

4 Choose the correct word to complete the sentences.

1 I _____ my parents $100.
   a refund   b owe   c pay back

2 We _____ them 2–1.
   a won   b scored   c beat

3 I'm not buying anything. I'm just _____ .
   a spending   b getting paid   c window shopping

4 You can only use your _____ to move the ball.
   a brain   b heart   c foot

5 Here's your change and here's your _____ .
   a cash   b refund   c receipt

6 There was a _____ of 60,000 at the game today.
   a spectator   b crowd   c athlete

7 How much do you _____ in your job?
   a earn   b be worth   c borrow

8 You need to _____ before a game.
   a cheat   b give up   c warm up

9 Look how long the _____ is!
   a line   b bargain   c cash register

10 The day after the marathon, my _____ ached!
   a cheek   b chin   c muscles

11 When I was younger, it was easy to touch my _____ , but now I can't.
   a toes   b fingers   c thumb

Personal Best

Lesson 9A — Name five things you can do with money.

Lesson 9A — Write two sentences about your grandparents using *used to*.

Lesson 9B — Name five things you usually see in a shopping mall.

Lesson 9C — Write two sentences in the passive: simple present and simple past.

Lesson 9D — Name five nouns ending in -*ion*.

Lesson 9D — Write an expression to start a formal e-mail, and another to end it.

Lesson 10A — Write a sentence using the past perfect.

Lesson 10A — Name three things you can win.

Lesson 10B — Write a sentence with *for example*, and another with *such as*.

Lesson 10C — Name five parts of the body that we have two of.

Lesson 10D — Give a phrase to start an inquiry, and another to ask for additional information.

Lesson 10D — Give an expression to check to make sure someone is satisfied.

93

UNIT 11 At home

LANGUAGE -*ing*/infinitive verb patterns ■ household items

11A Dream home

1 Look at the picture. Would you like to live somewhere like this? Why/Why not?

2 Read the text and answer the questions.
1 Where is the house?
2 Who are the people in the picture?
3 Why do they live there?

Living the dream

Have you ever imagined escaping city life and moving to a desert island? Well, meet the family who did just that.

Karyn von Engelbrechten wanted to travel the world after she became tired of her three-hour commute to London, where she worked as an IT manager. She left her job and her home and, with husband Boris and their three children, decided to start a new adventure.

They bought some land on a tiny island in the South Pacific and started to build a house with materials they found on the island. Everything was done by hand. They learned how to cut down trees to make floors and doors. Electricity was generated using solar panels, and rainwater was collected so the family had water in the bathrooms and kitchen. They even started growing their own fruit and vegetables.

Now the family runs their home as a guesthouse for other travelers. If you don't feel like swimming in the beautiful clear ocean, you can sit on the balcony and enjoy watching whales and turtles. The kitchen is basic, but it has most things you'd need, like a refrigerator and oven.

There's no air-conditioning, but the bedrooms are cool and comfortable, and there are extra blankets and comforters in the closet for the colder months. From the house, steps go down to your own private beach, or if you're feeling brave, you can explore the island.

It sounds like paradise, but there are some disadvantages. Apart from the fruit and vegetables that Karyn and Boris grow, they need to buy other things, and the nearest store is a three-hour boat trip away. The island is also very near a volcano, and they often have earthquakes and tropical storms. And their eldest son, Jack, has gone away to school in New Zealand because he missed being with other children his own age.

However, if you're tired of your daily routine, the message is clear—follow your dreams!

3 Which of these things does the house have? *Yes* (✓), *No* (X) or *Don't know* (?). Read the text again and check.

| 1 air-conditioning ☐ | 3 central heating ☐ | 5 refrigerator ☐ | 7 washing machine ☐ | 9 oven ☐ |
| 2 blankets ☐ | 4 dishwasher ☐ | 6 closet ☐ | 8 comforters ☐ | 10 faucets ☐ |

Go to Vocabulary practice: household items, page 154

4 A Ask and answer the questions in pairs.
1 Do you have a refrigerator or dishwasher at home?
2 How often do you use your washing machine?
3 How often do you use your iron? Do you like ironing?
4 Do you have a carpet or rugs in your home? What color are they?
5 Do you have a big closet? Is it well-organized or messy?
6 Do you sleep with a blanket or a comforter?
7 Do you have a microwave oven? How often do you use it?
8 Do you have central heating or air-conditioning in your home? How often do you turn it on?

B Tell the class some things you found out about your partner.

-ing/infinitive verb patterns ■ household items   **LANGUAGE**   **11A**

5 **A** Choose the correct form of the verbs to complete the sentences. Check your answers in the text.
1 Have you ever **imagined** *to escape / escaping* city life?
2 Karyn von Engelbrechten **wanted** *to travel / traveling* the world.
3 She **decided** *to start / starting* a new adventure.
4 You can sit on the balcony and **enjoy** *to watch / watching* whales and turtles.

B Answer the questions about the verbs in **bold** in sentences 1–4.
1 Which form of the verb comes after *imagine* and *enjoy*? Infinitive / *-ing* form
2 Which form of the verb comes after *want* and *decide*? Infinitive / *-ing* form

6 **A** Find examples of the verbs in the box in the text. Put them in the correct column.

manage   start   learn   feel like   need   miss

Verbs followed by *-ing*	Verbs followed by the infinitive

B Which verb can be followed by both the infinitive and the *-ing* form? _____
Now read the Grammar box.

> **Grammar** *-ing*/infinitive verb patterns
>
> Verbs followed by the *-ing* form: She **enjoys living** in the city.
> Verbs followed by the infinitive: I **want to live** in a bigger house.
>
> **Look!** Some verbs can be followed by both the infinitive and *-ing* forms:
> It started **to rain**. = It started **raining**.

Go to Grammar practice: *-ing*/infinitive verb patterns, page 132

7 ▶ 11.4 **Pronunciation:** sentence stress Listen and underline the stressed words in the sentences. How is *to* pronounced? Listen, check, and repeat.
1 Karyn wanted to travel the world.
2 She enjoys watching whales and turtles.

8 **A** Complete the sentences with the correct form of the verbs in parentheses.
1 She's planning _____ science. (study)
2 My doctor suggested _____ less coffee. (drink)
3 I haven't forgotten _____ the customer. (call)
4 Do you feel like _____ for pizza tonight? (go out)
5 We can't afford _____ on vacation. (go)
6 We should spend more time _____ . (study)

B ▶ 11.5 In pairs, practice saying the sentences. Pay attention to the sentence stress. Listen, check, and repeat.

Go to Communication practice: page 174

9 **A** Complete the questions with the correct form of the verbs in parentheses.
1 Imagine _____ (design) your dream house. What would you want it _____ (be) like?
2 Do you expect _____ (work) in the same job all your life? Are you planning _____ (change) jobs soon? What do you hope _____ (do) in the future?
3 Do you enjoy _____ (travel)? Are you planning _____ (go) anywhere soon?
4 Do you like _____ (live) in your house? What would you like _____ (change) about it?
5 Would you like _____ (live) abroad in the future? Where do feel like _____ (live)?
6 At what age do you think you will stop _____ (work)? What will you spend your time _____ (do) when you retire? Do you think you will miss _____ (work)?

B Ask and answer the questions in pairs.

Personal Best Write a description of a room in your house or apartment, including all the things in it.

11 SKILLS LISTENING understanding and interpreting information ■ omission of words ■ housework

11B The truth about housework

1 Look at the picture. Have you ever seen a kitchen like this? If so, where?

2 Complete the man's list of chores with the words in the box.

| do (x3)   clear   take out   load   mop   water   wash |

1 _____ the dishes   3 _____ the ironing   5 _____ the table   7 _____ the trash
2 _____ the dishwasher   4 _____ the laundry   6 _____ the plants   8 _____ the floor

Go to Vocabulary practice: housework, page 155

3 Complete the chart about you. In pairs, compare your charts and explain your answers.

Housework I hate doing	Housework I don't mind doing	Housework I enjoy doing

4 A ▶ 11.7   In pairs, decide if the sentences are true (T) or false (F). Watch or listen to the first part of *Learning Curve* and check.

1 It's a fact that everyone hates doing housework.   ____
2 The majority of us usually prefer to do other activities in our free time. ____
3 Today, robots that can do the housework for us really exist.   ____
4 Robots will never have arms and legs.   ____
5 In Japan, there's a robot that can pick up heavy things.   ____

B ▶ 11.7   Watch or listen again. Write down the key words that Simon or Kate use that helped you check the answers.

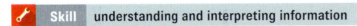

Skill   understanding and interpreting information

It's helpful to notice key words and phrases before you listen.
• Look at the questions and underline any key words or phrases.
• Think about other words or phrases that speakers could use to give this information.
• As you listen, pay attention to all the words and phrases you have noticed or thought of.

96

understanding and interpreting information ■ omission of words ■ housework   **LISTENING**   SKILLS   **11B**

5 **A** Look at the underlined key words in questions 1 and 2 and think about what words and phrases Julie might use. Underline the key words in questions 3-6.

B ▶ 11.8 Watch or listen to the second part of the show. Choose the correct options.

1 What does Julie prefer doing on the weekend?
  a She prefers <u>spending time</u> with her <u>children</u>.
  b She prefers going <u>shopping</u>.
  c She prefers doing <u>housework</u>.
2 Why does she want her children to do housework?
  a She has <u>too much work</u>.
  b So they <u>learn</u> to do things <u>on their own</u>.
  c Because it's <u>healthier</u> than <u>video games</u>.
3 Why did Axel buy a cleaning robot?
  a He wants more time for himself.
  b The salesperson offered him a good price.
  c He injured his back.
4 What does he say about his dishwasher?
  a It's broken.
  b He prefers washing the dishes by hand.
  c It works very well.
5 Why does Roberta buy the "Mop It" robot?
  a It's better at cleaning than she is.
  b Her friend has one.
  c There was a discount.
6 How does housework help her?
  a It's a way to get exercise.
  b It helps her relax.
  c She saves money.

Julie

Axel

Roberta

6 Discuss the questions in pairs.

1 Do you share the housework equally at home?
2 Who does the most housework? Why?
3 Did you do housework when you were a child?
4 Do you think doing housework is good for you?

7 ▶ 11.9 Read and listen to the phrases from the show. Which words are missing? Why didn't the speakers use them?

1 Just doing a bit of dusting in the studio.
2 Anyone there with an opinion?
3 Makes the floor look good.
4 It does a better job than I can. So exciting!

Listening builder   omission of words

Speakers sometimes don't say all the words in a sentence because they think the meaning is obvious without them, or because they don't want to repeat words or phrases.

Pronouns: *No, (I) don't really like cleaning.*
Articles: *(The) Dishwasher's broken.*
be and auxiliary verbs: *(It's) Time for spring cleaning.*
There is/are: *(Is there) Anyone there with an opinion?*
Avoid repeating words: *It does a better job than I can (do).*
Phrases: *Anyway, (let's go) back to Kate.*

8 A ▶ 11.10 Read the Listening builder. Read and listen to the conversation. Which words are missing?

Mario Hi, Maya. ¹_____ You there?
Maya   ²_____ In the living room. ³_____ Just clearing the table.
Mario ⁴_____ Coffee's ready. ⁵_____ Want some?
Maya   No, thanks. ⁶_____ Already had three ⁷_____ today.

B ▶ 11.11 Listen and check.

9 In pairs, discuss the statement: "People only notice housework when it isn't done."

Personal Best   Write a short conversation about housework where the speakers omit words.

97

11 LANGUAGE articles ■ words to describe materials and clothes

11C Technology you can wear

1 Discuss the questions in pairs.
  1 Do you find it difficult to decide what to wear each day?
  2 How often do you buy new clothes?
  3 What are your favorite clothes in your closet?

2 Label the picture with the materials in the box.

| cotton   leather   wood   denim   wool   metal |

Go to Vocabulary practice: words to describe materials and clothes, page 156

3 In pairs, describe the different types of clothes.

- what you're wearing now
- what you wear on the weekend
- what you'd wear to a wedding
- what you'd wear to a party
- what you'd wear to a job interview
- what you'd wear on a first date

4 Look at pictures a–c. What do they show? Read the text and match them with descriptions 1–3.

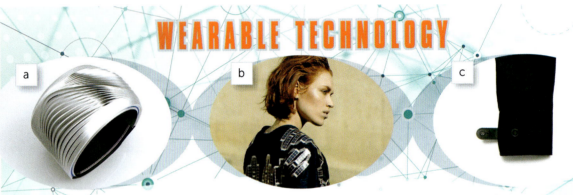

WEARABLE TECHNOLOGY

Our houses are full of technology, but how much do we have in our closets? You might think you don't have any, but get ready for that to change. Experts predict that the amount of money we spend on wearable technology will reach $74 billion a year by 2025. You're probably already familiar with smart watches and fitness bracelets, but what are some of the other things coming our way?

1 MATERIAL THAT CAN COMMUNICATE

In the U.S., Google and Levi's® are developing a new kind of material that is touch sensitive, like the screen on a smartphone. The material is made by running thin metal wires through cotton, denim, or silk. Designers can then use this material to create interactive areas on clothes and furniture. Soon people will be able to control machines just by touching their pants legs!

2 ACCESSORIES THAT CONTROL YOUR TEMPERATURE

Have you ever been in a place where half the people are complaining about the cold, and the other half are too hot? The solution is *Wristify*, a bracelet that can heat or cool your skin at the touch of a button. It's perfect for a trip to the gym, a day at the beach, or for keeping you warm at home. In fact, the bracelet could also save you money on energy bills. The design isn't finished yet, but here's what the final product might look like.

3 CLOTHES THAT CHARGE YOUR PHONE

Pauline van Dongen is an exciting new designer who specializes in wearable technology, and uses both traditional and new materials to create amazing clothes. Her stylish T-shirts and jackets have solar panels that can charge a cell phone in just a few hours ... when the sun is shining, of course.

5 Discuss the questions in pairs.
  1 Which idea do you think is the most useful? Why?
  2 Would you buy any of these inventions? Why/Why not?
  3 Can you think of other types of wearable technology?

98

articles ■ words to describe materials and clothes **LANGUAGE** **11C**

6 Complete the sentences with the articles *a, an, the,* or – (no article). Check your answers in the text.

1 The amount of money we spend on wearable technology will reach $74 billion ____ year.
2 People will be able to control ____ machines just by touching their pants legs!
3 The solution is *Wristify,* ____ bracelet that can heat or cool your skin.
4 Perfect for a trip to ____ gym…
5 … or for keeping you warm at ____ home.
6 ____ bracelet could also save you money on energy bills.
7 Pauline van Dongen is ____ exciting new designer.
8 … when ____ sun is shining, of course.

7 Match sentences 1–8 in exercise 6 with rules a–h. Then read the Grammar box.

a We use *a/an* to talk about a person or thing for the first time. ____
b We use *the* when we have already mentioned the person or thing before. ____
c We don't use an article to talk about things in general (plural or uncountable nouns). ____
d We use *a/an* to talk about a person's job. ____
e We use *a/an* in some measurement expressions. ____
f We use *the* if there is only one of the thing. ____
g We use *the* with specific places in a town. ____
h We don't use an article with some places we go to regularly. ____

📖 **Grammar** **articles**

a/an	*the*	No article
*I live in **a** tall apartment building.*	*I live in a modern apartment. **The** apartment is in …*	*They're interested in sports cars.*
*Eric is **an** architect.*	*The address is on **the** Internet.*	*I leave for work at about 9:00 a.m.*
*We go sailing twice **a** month.*	*I'll meet you in **the** park.*	*We go on vacation every summer.*

Personal Best

Go to Grammar practice: articles, page 133

8 A ▶11.15 **Pronunciation:** *the* Listen and repeat the phrases. Match the words in **bold** with the sounds /ðə/ and /ði/. Why does the pronunciation change?

1 **the** amount of money we spend on technology ____   2 **the** screen on a smartphone ____

B ▶11.16 Practice saying the words in pairs. Pay attention to the pronunciation of *the*. Listen, check, and repeat.

the solution   the answer   the office   the U.S.   the Internet   the sun   the hour   the gym

Go to Communication practice: Student A, page 165; Student B, page 173

9 ▶11.17 Complete the text with *a, an, the,* or – (no article). Listen and check.

A BRIGHT IDEA

Christina Mercando is [1]____ businesswoman and [2]____ inventor. She started [3]____ company in [4]____ U.S. named Ringly. Her first product was [5]____ ring that connects to your smartphone. When [6]____ phone receives [7]____ text or e-mail, [8]____ ring lights up. [9]____ idea came to Christina when she was having [10]____ dinner with friends. She didn't want to miss any important calls on her phone, but she didn't want to put her phone on [11]____ dinner table. It's [12]____ common problem for [13]____ women who keep [14]____ phones in their handbags or purses, where they may not hear them. [15]____ rings are made in China, and Christina talks with the factory once [16]____ week. It's [17]____ exciting time for Christina, and [18]____ future is definitely bright!

10 In pairs, take turns talking about these things. Remember to use the correct articles.

kinds of food and drink you hate	a machine that you couldn't live without	the places you went to yesterday
what you have in your bedroom	some clothes you want to buy, but can't afford	how often you charge your cell phone

Personal Best Think of an idea for another piece of wearable technology. Write about how it could work.

99

11 SKILLS WRITING making writing interesting ■ adjective order

11D House exchange

1 Discuss the questions in pairs.
1 Have you ever done a house exchange or stayed at someone else's house on vacation?
2 What are the advantages and disadvantages of a house exchange?
3 How would you feel about letting strangers stay in your home?

2 Describe the pictures. Which home would you prefer to stay in? Why?

a

b

3 Read the description on a house exchange website. Which home from exercise 2 does it describe?

 Homes away from home | Two-bedroom apartment in downtown Chicago

About our home

Our home is an attractive two-bedroom apartment, very near downtown Chicago. It's a 20-minute walk from the Willis Tower, where there is an amazing view of the city.

The main bedroom has its own bathroom and a double bed with plain white cotton sheets. Although the second bedroom is slightly smaller, it's bright and has two comfortable single beds. There's a fashionable leather sofa and two large armchairs in the modern living room. The spacious, up-to-date kitchen includes everything you'll need, including an electric oven, refrigerator, freezer, dishwasher, and a new Italian coffeemaker. Glass doors open from the kitchen onto a gorgeous, sunny balcony, where you can have a relaxing breakfast.

The apartment is on a peaceful street, but it's just a few minutes away from Chicago's famous Miracle Mile, known for it stores, hotels, and some excellent restaurants. The train station is also close by, so this is an ideal place if you want to explore all of Chicago's attractions.

7 reviews
★★★★

2 bedrooms

Sleeps 4

2 bathrooms

4 A Read the text again. Find words that mean the same as adjectives 1–6.

1 big   _____
2 beautiful   _____
3 quiet   _____
4 very good   _____
5 light   _____
6 modern   _____

B How does the writer make the text interesting? Read the Skill box.

🔧 Skill making writing interesting

We can use different techniques to make our writing more interesting.
- Use a variety of adjectives to describe things: *a **gorgeous**, **sunny** balcony*
- Use synonyms to avoid repeating words: *two **large** armchairs, the **spacious** kitchen*
- Use linkers to give reasons and results (*so, because, that's why*), to contrast information (*but, although, however*) or add information (*and, also, too, as well*).
- When you describe a place, use *where* and an example of what you can do: *a balcony, where you can have a relaxing breakfast*

making writing interesting ■ adjective order   **WRITING**   **SKILLS** **11D**

5 In pairs, rewrite the sentences to make them more interesting.

1 The house is very pretty. It has a pretty yard.
The house is very pretty, and it has a gorgeous yard.

2 The apartment is fairly small. It's a good place to stay. It's right downtown.
_____

3 There's an old living room. It has an old fireplace. You can stay warm in the winter.
_____

4 The building has a quiet roof terrace. You can enjoy nice views of the countryside.
_____

5 If the weather is nice, you can sit in the big yard.
_____

6 Complete the phrases with the adjectives in parentheses in the correct order. Check your answers in the text.

1 an _____ _____ apartment (two-bedroom, attractive)
2 _____ _____ _____ sheets (cotton, plain, white)
3 a _____ _____ sofa (fashionable, leather)
4 a _____ _____ coffeemaker (Italian, new)

⊞ Text builder   adjective order

When we use more than one adjective to describe a noun, they go in a specific order:
opinion   size   shape   age   color   nationality   material   (noun)
She has long blond hair. NOT ~~She has blond long hair~~.
It's an interesting Chinese painting. NOT ~~It's a Chinese interesting painting~~.

7 Read the Text builder. Put the words in the box in the correct columns.

blue   Dutch   glass   green   large   leather   Mexican   old
round   small   square   stylish   unusual   young

opinion	size	shape	age	color	nationality	material

8 Complete the sentences with the adjectives in parentheses in the correct order.

1 We live in a _____ _____ _____ house in the country. (stone, beautiful, old)
2 It has _____ _____ floors, and is warm and cozy. (wood, attractive)
3 There's a _____ _____ rug on the floor. (square, wool)
4 You can relax on one of our _____ _____ _____ armchairs. (leather, old, comfortable)
5 Outside, there's a _____ _____ garden. (Japanese, beautiful)
6 Near the house, there's a _____ _____ restaurant. (Indian, fantastic)

9 Write descriptions of three items you own, using as many adjectives as possible. Compare with a partner.
I have a beautiful old brown leather armchair.

10 **A PREPARE** Plan a description of your home or apartment for a home exchange website. Write notes for three paragraphs:

Paragraph 1: the type of home it is and where it is
Paragraph 2: description of the rooms and what is in the rooms
Paragraph 3: description of the local area and what is nearby

B PRACTICE Write your description. Remember to order adjectives correctly.

C PERSONAL BEST Exchange texts with a partner. After reading the description, would you like to stay there? How could he/she make the description more interesting?

Personal Best   Write a short description of a place you know well, such as where you work or study, a restaurant, or a store.   101

UNIT 12 People and relationships

LANGUAGE defining relative clauses ■ relationships

12A Bring your parents to work

1   Match the words in the box with the definitions.

| colleague | neighbor | in-laws | boss | roommate |
| employee | business partner | relative | | |

1 someone who manages you at work _____
2 your husband's/wife's mother and father _____
3 someone who works for you _____
4 someone in your family _____
5 someone who works with you _____
6 someone who lives near you _____
7 someone who shares an apartment with you _____
8 someone who owns a company with you _____

Go to Vocabulary practice: relationships, page 157

2   Choose three of the relationships from exercise 1 and write down the names of people you know. Tell your partner about them.

3   Read the text and answer the questions.
1 Which company introduced the idea of a *Bring Your Parents to Work Day*?
2 How many people in the U.S. take part in the *Take Your Child to Work Day*?
3 What does the company say the benefits of the day are?
4 How many companies now have a similar day?
5 What does Martin Richards' daughter do at work?

Would you bring your parents to work?

How would you feel about bringing your mom or dad to work with you? Would you be worried about the things that they might say to your boss? Or nervous that they might start showing embarrassing photos of you as a child to the co-worker who sits next to you? Well, get ready for *Bring Your Parents to Work Day*, an event that is already becoming popular in some U.S. companies and that could be coming your way soon!

The company where it all started, LinkedIn, realized that there are a lot of parents who don't understand what their children's jobs involve. There is already a national *Take Your Child to Work Day* for workers who want to take their sons and daughters to their places of work, and more than 37 million Americans take part every year. So why not do the same thing for parents? LinkedIn's argument is that employees who feel supported by their family are happier and more productive. Now, there are more than 80 companies in 18 countries that organize an annual event for parents to get to know how their kids spend their time at work.
So what do the parents think of it? Martin Richards has just spent a day at the office where his daughter and son-in-law work. "For me, it was a great opportunity to see how digital marketing works, to meet some of Imogen's co-workers, and, best of all, to spend a day with my eldest daughter!"

102

defining relative clauses ■ relationships   LANGUAGE 12A

4 Discuss the questions in pairs.
1 As a child, did you ever visit the place where your parents worked? Was it a useful experience?
2 How would you feel if you brought your parents to your place of work? Why?
3 Do you think people's jobs have changed a lot in the last thirty years? If so, how?

5 A Complete the sentences with *who*, *that*, or *where*. Check your answers in the text.
1 Get ready for *Bring Your Parents to Work Day*, an event _____ is already becoming popular in some U.S. companies.
2 There is already a national *Take Your Child to Work Day* for workers _____ want to take their sons and daughters to their places of work.
3 Martin Richards has just spent a day at the office _____ his daughter and son-in-law work.

B Look at sentences 1–3 and answer the questions. Then read the Grammar box.
1 Which word do we use to give information about: people? _____ things? _____ places? _____
2 In which sentence can we use *that* instead? ____

Grammar defining relative clauses

To give information about people: I'm going to see my cousin **who** lives in Greece.
All employees **that** work in the sales department have a meeting.
To give information about things: The company sells machines **that** are made in Japan.
It looks like the shirt **(that)** my roommate bought last week.
To give information about places: That's the restaurant **where** my brother-in-law works.

Go to Grammar practice: defining relative clauses, page 134

6 A ▶12.3 **Pronunciation:** sentence stress Listen to the sentences and underline the stressed words. When do we stress *who*?
1 Who do you live with?
2 The man who works at the bank.

B ▶12.4 Match the halves to make sentences. Listen, check, and repeat. Pay attention to the sentence stress.
1 A remote control is something that
2 A flight attendant is someone who
3 A kindergarten is a place where

a young children go.
b you use to turn on the TV.
c works on a plane.

7 A Write definitions with *who*, *where*, or *that*.
1 something / use to see small things
_____
2 a place / buy newspapers and magazines
_____
3 someone / collects the garbage
_____
4 an animal / very slow and lives in trees
_____
5 a person / plays an instrument on the street
_____
6 a building / horses sleep and eat
_____

  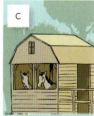

B In pairs, match definitions 1–6 with pictures a–f. Do you know the names of these things in English?

Go to Communication practice: Student A, page 165; Student B, page 173

8 Complete the sentences so that they are true for you. Compare your sentences in pairs.
1 I like going on vacation to places where …
2 Most of my friends are people who …
3 I like TV shows that …
4 I wouldn't want to live in an area where …
5 The worst kind of boss is someone who …
6 I don't like food that …

Personal Best Write about a friend, a relative, or a co-worker. Use relative clauses to describe him/her.

103

12 SKILLS READING interpreting data ■ expressing approximate quantities

12B In our lifetime

1 In pairs, write down five activities that take up the most time on a typical day.

sleeping, working ...

2 Look at Chart 1 on page 105. Answer the questions.

1 What are the top five activities in the pie chart?
2 Are they similar to your list in exercise 1?
3 What information does the pie chart show?
4 Does anything surprise you?

Skill interpreting data

Many texts include graphs and charts to show information more clearly.
- Read any words on the graphs like the title, the key, and the horizontal and vertical axes.
- Look at the data and think about the information it shows.
- When you read a paragraph, look at the graph or chart it describes again and see how the words relate to the data.
- Use information in the text and the graphs and charts to answer the questions.

3 **A** Read the Skill box. Look at Graphs 1 and 2. What do they show?

B Choose the correct options to complete the information about Graphs 2 and 3.
1 We spend *more / less* time at work than in the past.
2 Over the last twenty years, there *has / hasn't* been a big change.
3 The total time spent on housework by men and women has *decreased / increased*.
4 Men do *more / less* housework now than in 1965.

4 Read the text and look at Chart 1 and Graphs 1 and 2. Check (✓) the best summary of the text.
1 We have a lot more time to spend with friends and family than in the past. ☐
2 We worked more in the past, but we were happier. ☐
3 We have very busy lives and not much time to do the important things. ☐

5 Read the text and look at Chart 1 and Graphs 1 and 2 again. Are the sentences true (T) or false (F)?
1 On average, people live to be 76 years old. ____
2 In 1900, people worked 60 hours a week. ____
3 We spend about a third of our lives sleeping. ____
4 We spend two and a half years in the shower. ____
5 People who work in big cities spend less than a year in their cars. ____
6 We spend a lot of free time using technology. ____

6 Do you think the information is correct for people in your country? Why/Why not? Discuss in pairs.

Text builder expressing approximate quantities

Approximately: During a typical lifetime, we spend **around** 91,000 hours at work.
People sleep for **about** eight hours a day.
That means we spend **roughly** three and a half years of our lives studying.
More than: ... just **over** two years to spend with family and friends.
The same/more: You can say goodbye to **at least** another year of your life.
Less than: ... which is **nearly** ten and a half years.   We spend **almost** four years using our phones.

7 Read the Text builder. Write sentences about how much time you spend doing the activities in the boxes. Use words to express approximate quantities.

104

interpreting data ■ expressing approximate quantities READING SKILLS 12B

Where does the time go?

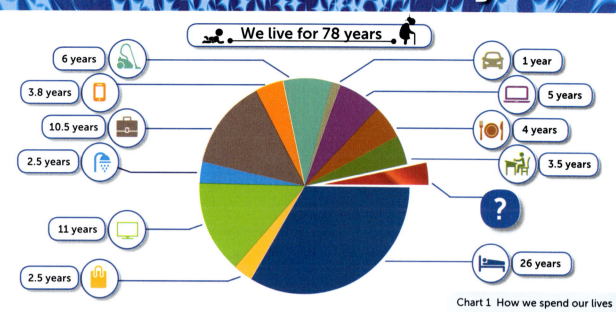

Chart 1 How we spend our lives

We have more free time than ever before. In many countries, the average working week is now under 40 hours, far shorter than it was for our parents and grandparents before us. So why do our lives feel so busy, and where does our time go?

Graph 1

People sleep for about eight hours a day, which means we spend 26 years in our beds, in an average lifetime of 78 years. We spend another eleven years watching TV and, depending on where you live, two years of that can be spent just watching the commercials!

In a typical lifetime, we spend around 91,000 hours at work, which is nearly ten and a half years. And do you drive to work? If so, you can say goodbye to at least another year of your life—even more if you work in a big city like Istanbul or Rio de Janeiro and have to sit in traffic jams every day.

In many countries, the law requires young people to stay in school until they're at least 16 years old. Many go on to higher education at a university or college. That means we spend, on average, 31,000 hours—roughly three and a half years of our lives—studying. Two and a half years of our lives are spent in the bathroom, brushing our teeth, using the toilet, taking a shower, and getting ready to go out. Shopping uses up another two and a half years, and we spend at least another four years eating.

The introduction of modern appliances, such as dishwashers, washing machines, and microwaves, means that, overall, we spend less time cooking and cleaning than our parents did. Women still do most of the housework, but men are sharing domestic tasks more than they used to.

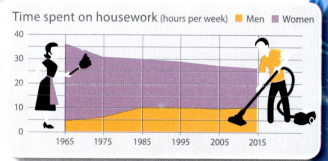

Graph 2

In recent years, the biggest change in how we spend our time is technology. We spend an average of five years online and almost four years using our phones, and those numbers are increasing every year.

If you add up all that time, it leaves you with just over two years on average to spend with family and friends, to see the world, and to achieve your dreams. So, what are you waiting for? The clock is ticking!

Personal Best Make a pie chart and write about how you spend your time on the weekend.

105

12 LANGUAGE — uses of the -ing form and the infinitive ■ relationship verbs

12C Long-distance love

1 Look at the pictures and the title. Answer the questions in pairs. Then read the text and check.

1. What do you think the text is about?
2. Where do you think the man is?
3. Where do you think the woman is?
4. How do you think they stay in touch?

The ultimate long-distance relationship

Having a long-distance relationship isn't easy. Staying in touch takes extra effort, and not having your partner around when you need support can be difficult. So it's hard to imagine what life is like for Amiko Kauderer, whose boyfriend, Scott Kelly, is often not even on the planet with her. That's because Scott is an astronaut who spends months floating 400 km. above the Earth on the International Space Station!

Amiko works at NASA, which is how she got to know Scott. They met a few times, and after talking "for hours and hours" one evening, Scott finally asked her out. They've now been together for several years. However, Scott's job means he is often away. His first trip to the Space Station lasted six months. After that, he lived in space for a whole year to find out what would happen to the human body on a journey to Mars. On his first trip, it wasn't easy for Amiko to stay in touch. E-mailing involved a six-hour delay, but now it's almost instant, and it's also possible to videochat once a week. But there are some things that can't be done. "One of the things I miss most is holding hands," says Amiko. "We can connect by phone. I can upload pictures, but you can't upload human touch."

Other couples might have broken up in such a situation, but not Scott and Amiko. "We really appreciate a challenge because we know that in the end, we will be able to say, 'Yeah, we did that'."

So, whenever you think your love life is difficult, just think of Amiko and Scott!

2 A Match sentences 1–5 with pictures a–e.

1. Amiko **got to know** Scott at a friend's house. ____
2. They **fell in love** at first sight. ____
3. Scott **asked** Amiko **out** on a date. ____
4. **Staying in touch** now is easier than it was. ____
5. They **broke up**, but **got back together** in the end. ____

B Are the sentences true (T) or false (F)? Check your answers in the text.

Go to Vocabulary practice: relationship verbs, page 157

uses of the *-ing* form and the infinitive ■ relationship verbs **LANGUAGE 12C**

3 Choose the correct words to complete the sentences. Check your answers in the text.
1 *Have / Having* a long-distance relationship isn't easy.
2 ... after *to talk / talking* "for hours and hours" one evening, Scott finally asked her out.
3 He lived in space for a whole year *to find out / finding out* what would happen to the human body.
4 It's also possible *to videochat / videochatting* once a week.

4 Look at sentences 1–4 from exercise 3 again. Complete the rules with the *-ing* form or infinitive. Then read the Grammar box.
1 We use _____ after an adjective.
2 We usually use _____ as the subject/object of a sentence.
3 We use _____ after a preposition.
4 We use _____ to say why we did something.

Grammar   uses of the *-ing* form and the infinitive

-ing form of the verb:
After a preposition: I'm interested **in learning** languages.
Subject/object of a sentence: **Breaking up** with someone is hard.   I hate **breaking up** with someone.
Infinitive:
After an adjective: It's **difficult to meet** new people in this city.   It's **important to stay** in touch.
To express a purpose: I went to Juan's house **to talk** to him.

Go to Grammar practice: uses of the *-ing* form and the infinitive, page 135

5 A ▶ 12.7 **Pronunciation:** word stress Listen to the words and underline the stressed syllables. Listen again, check, and repeat.
1 distance   2 relationship   3 imagine   4 happen

B ▶ 12.8 Underline the stressed syllables in the words below. Listen, check, and repeat.
important   colleagues   impossible   except   technology   better   afraid   probably

6 A ▶ 12.9 Write the infinitive or the *-ing* form of the verbs in parentheses. Listen and check.
1 It's very important _____ with your colleagues at work. (get along)
2 _____ in love at first sight is impossible, except in the movies. (fall)
3 You can use technology _____ in touch, but meeting face to face is better. (stay)
4 You shouldn't be afraid of _____ someone out. He or she will probably say yes! (ask)

B In pairs, practice saying sentences 1–4. Say if you agree or disagree with the sentences.

Go to Communication practice: Student A, page 165; Student B, page 173

7 Complete the text with the infinitive or the *-ing* form of the verbs in the box.

arrive   choose   say   make   show

HOW TO SUCCEED ON A FIRST DATE

1 _____ a nice place to meet is the first thing you need to think about.
2 You should wear nice clothes _____ a good impression.
3 It's important _____ on time.
4 Don't be afraid of _____ the real you.
5 Before _____ good night, tell him/her that you enjoyed the date.

8 In pairs, think of more advice for how to succeed on a first date. Use the ideas in the boxes.

| be polite | don't talk too much | ask questions | make eye contact | laugh | listen | smile | tell a joke | relax |

A *I think it's important to be polite.*   **B** *Yes, but being polite isn't the most important thing ...*

Personal Best Write a paragraph about a couple you know. Explain how they met and their relationship.

12 SKILLS SPEAKING saying thanks ■ responding modestly

12D Thanks a million!

a   b   c   d

1 A Look at the pictures. How are the people celebrating their birthday?

B Answer the questions.
1 How important are birthdays to you? Why?
2 How did you celebrate your last birthday?
3 What's the best birthday present you've ever received? Why?
4 Have you ever had a surprise birthday party? Did you enjoy it?

2 ▶12.10 Watch or listen to the first part of *Learning Curve*. Are the sentences true (T) or false (F)?
1 Today is Simon's birthday. ____
2 Everyone has forgotten about his birthday. ____
3 Simon has a tennis match today. ____
4 Kate gives Simon a present. ____
5 Simon will pay to post the parcel. ____
6 Simon's parents always call him in the morning. ____

3 A ▶12.10 Watch or listen again. Match the phrases 1–5 with the reasons a–e.
1 That's very kind of you.   a Kate gives Simon a cup of tea.
2 Thanks a lot.   b Kate offers to make Simon tea.
3 Thanks so much!   c Simon says he'll pay at the post office.
4 Thanks a million!   d Simon agrees to post a parcel.
5 I will, thanks.   e Kate wants Simon to say hello to his parents for her.

B Look at phrases 1–5 again. Answer the questions.
1 Which phrases are polite responses to something small? ____ ____
2 Which phrases are used to say thanks for something special or a big effort? ____ ____ ____
3 Can you think of any other ways to thank someone?

Conversation builder   saying thanks

To be polite:	For a special favor:	To be more formal:
Thanks a lot.	*That's very nice/kind of you.*	*I can't thank you enough.*
Thanks very much.	*Thanks a million.*	*I'm so grateful to you.*
Thanks.	*Thank you so much.*	*We really appreciate it.*

4 ▶12.11 Read the Conversation builder. In pairs, read the sentences out loud and thank your partner in an appropriate way. Listen and compare your answers.

1 Here's your T-shirt and $1 change.
2 We've decided to give you a 30% pay raise.
3 Here are some flowers. I know you've been sick.
4 The bus station? It's right across the street.
5 I've done all the shopping for you.
6 I cooked spaghetti. It's your favorite.

108

saying thanks ■ responding modestly **SPEAKING**   SKILLS **12D**

5 ▶ 12.12 Watch or listen to the second part of the show. What other ways of thanking people do you hear?

6 ▶ 12.12 Answer the questions. Watch or listen again and check.
1 Who cooked the food for the party? _____
2 Who sent flowers, chocolate, and biscuits? _____
3 Did Kate organize the party on her own? _____
4 Whose parents arrive at the party? _____

7 ▶ 12.13 Complete the sentences with the phrases in the box. Listen, check, and repeat after the beeps.

it was easy   Glad you noticed   You're welcome   I had help   it isn't a problem

1 **Kate**   Oh, and thanks again for taking this parcel.
  Simon Really, _____ .
2 **Simon** You look great, Pen. Is that a new dress?
  Penny Thanks. _____ !
3 **Penny** Jack, you really made a fantastic meal!
  Jack   Oh, come on, _____ . I make this all the time.
4 **Simon** Lovely. I'm so grateful to you both!
  Penny It was nothing. _____ .
5 **Simon** That was a fantastic surprise. Kate, did you do all this by yourself?
  Kate   No, _____ !

🔧 **Skill** responding modestly

We often respond to congratulations, thanks, and compliments in a modest way.
• For congratulations, you can say it wasn't important or hard work, e.g., *It was nothing, I was just lucky.*
• For thanks, you can say it was something small or you enjoyed doing it, e.g., *No problem. It was a pleasure. You're welcome.*
• For a compliment, you can thank the person and say you are pleased, e.g., *Thanks. I'm glad you like it.* You can also say it's not as good as the person thinks, e.g., *This old thing? I've had it for years.*

8 ▶ 12.14 Read the Skill box. Match phrases 1–6 with responses a–f. Listen and check.
1 I can't thank you enough.
2 I love your new hairstyle.
3 This chicken is delicious.
4 You passed! Congratulations.
5 Thanks for taking care of my children.
6 Congratulations on your promotion.

a Really? I thought it was too spicy.
b Oh, it's just an small one.
c Thanks. I'm glad you noticed.
d It was a pleasure. They're lots of fun!
e Thanks. The exam wasn't that difficult.
f It's no problem.

Go to Communication practice: Student A, page 165; Student B, page 173

9 A PREPARE In pairs, look at the pictures and choose a situation. Prepare a short conversation between the people.

 a
 b
 c
 d

B PRACTICE Act out your conversation to another pair.

C PERSONAL BEST What was good about the other pair's conversation? What could they do better? Change partners and prepare a conversation for another situation.

Personal Best Make a list of people you have thanked this week and explain why you thanked them.

11 and 12 REVIEW and PRACTICE

Grammar

1 Choose the correct options to complete the sentences.

1 Kevin has decided _____ his job.
  a quit
  b to quit
  c quitting

2 I usually go to _____ bed at 11:00 p.m.
  a a
  b the
  c – (no article)

3 Do you want _____ out tonight?
  a go
  b to go
  c going

4 My sister is _____ lawyer.
  a a
  b the
  c – (no article)

5 I'm getting together with a colleague _____ just left the company.
  a where
  b what
  c who

6 I called him _____ a meeting.
  a arrange
  b to arrange
  c arranging

7 This is the café _____ we said we would meet.
  a where
  b who
  c that

8 I'm crazy about _____ to other countries.
  a travel
  b to travel
  c traveling

2 Complete the sentences with the correct form of the verbs in the box.

| remember take buy find |
| go work meet write |

1 I went to the library _____ a book about pets.
2 I'm not happy about _____ late this week.
3 He forgot _____ his girlfriend a birthday present.
4 I've finally finished _____ my essay.
5 I can't stand _____ the subway. It's so crowded!
6 She's suggested _____ to the movies tonight.
7 It's important _____ to turn off this machine when you leave.
8 _____ you is the best thing that has happened to me!

3 Choose the correct options to complete the text.

Stephanie is ¹*a / - / the* wedding planner and she is ²*an / - / the* owner of *Blissful Days*, ³*a / - / the* company based in Sydney, Australia.

How did you become a wedding planner?

I've always loved ⁴*go / to go / going* to weddings. It's so exciting ⁵*see / to see / seeing* everyone dressed up and enjoying such a wonderful day. But I noticed that some people couldn't enjoy it because they were worried about ⁶*organize / to organize / organizing* everything. That's when I realized that I could start a company ⁷*that / who / where* helps people plan their weddings.

What advice can you give to couples planning a wedding?

First of all, you should agree on the guests ⁸*what / – / where* you're going to invite. Once you know how many people will be there, you can find a place ⁹*who / that / where* everyone will be comfortable. Send out invitations at least six months before the wedding, but expect that about 20% of people won't be able to attend. There could be more if the date of your wedding is on or near ¹⁰*a / - / the* legal holiday, so always check your dates carefully.

Vocabulary

1 Match the words in the box with the definitions.

| oven get back together plain do the laundry |
| hang out the clothes groom stylish iron |
| go out together roommate |

1 a machine you use to make clothes flat _____
2 a man who is going to get married _____
3 to start a relationship with someone _____
4 simple, with no pattern or design _____
5 someone who you live with _____
6 a machine you use to cook food _____
7 to dry clothes after you wash them _____
8 to wash your clothes _____
9 fashionable and elegant _____
10 to return to a relationship with someone _____

REVIEW and PRACTICE 11 and 12

2 Circle the words that are different. Explain your answers.

1 employer | classmate | colleague | business partner
2 break up | fall in love | go on a date | go out together
3 oven | dishwasher | sink | washing machine
4 mop | sweep | iron | vacuum
5 loose | wool | tight | casual
6 bride | girlfriend | stepsister | father-in-law
7 formal | cotton | denim | silk
8 sheets | pillow | comforter | iron
9 along well | married | in love | back together
10 wash the dishes | set the table | make the bed | load the dishwasher

3 Choose the correct word to complete the sentences.

1 My uncle's daughter is my _____ .
   a niece   b cousin   c stepsister
2 I am _____ . I don't have any brothers or sisters.
   a an only child   b a single parent   c a relative
3 I quit my job because I _____ badly with my boss.
   a got back   b got along   c went along
4 He _____ on a date!
   a introduced   b asked me out   c stayed in touch
5 The _____ is broken. Can you call a plumber?
   a oven   b faucet   c refrigerator
6 We need new _____ for the bed.
   a rugs   b carpets   c sheets
7 I don't know him. He's a complete _____ .
   a twin   b enemy   c stranger
8 It's really hot today. Can you _____ the plants?
   a sweep   b dust   c water

4 Complete the conversation with the words in the box.

> get to know   break up   vacuum
> introduce   nice   do   silk   mop

Sue When did you ¹ _____ with Harry?
Jo Two months ago.
Sue Let me ² _____ you to Lee. I'm meeting him tonight.
Jo I can't. I have to ³ _____ the carpets and ⁴ _____ the floor.
Sue You can do that any time!
Jo But I don't have anything to wear. I need to ⁵ _____ the laundry!
Sue Is your ⁶ _____ dress clean?
Jo Yes, it is.
Sue Well, that's really ⁷ _____ . Wear that! Come on, you should ⁸ _____ him. He's wonderful!
Jo OK, I'll come with you.

Personal Best

Lesson 11A
Name five objects you can find in a kitchen.

Lesson 12A
Write down five people, and say how you are related to each of them.

Lesson 11A
Name five verbs that are followed by the *-ing* form.

Lesson 12A
Write three sentences with relative clauses and *who, that,* and *where.*

Lesson 11B
Name five household chores you do at home.

Lesson 12B
Write three sentences using *roughly, at least,* and *almost.*

Lesson 11C
Write a sentence with *a/an,* and another with *the.*

Lesson 12C
Write a sentence with the infinitive.

Lesson 11C
Use adjectives to describe two things you are wearing now.

Lesson 12D
Give three expressions to thank someone.

Lesson 11D
Describe a noun using three adjectives in the correct order.

Lesson 12D
Give an expression for responding modestly when someone thanks you.

111

GRAMMAR PRACTICE

7A Present perfect with *yet* and *already*

We often use the present perfect with *yet* and *already*.

Have you been to the new café yet?
Yes, I've already been there.
No, I haven't been there yet.

We use *yet* in negative sentences and questions to talk about something that we expected to happen before now. *Yet* comes at the end of the sentence or question.

Have you written the report yet?
I haven't finished it yet.

We use *already* to talk about something that happened before now or earlier than we expected. *Already* comes before the main verb.

Do you want to go out for lunch?
No, thanks. I've already eaten.

We sometimes use *already* in questions instead of *yet*. *Already* comes between the auxiliary verb and the main verb or at the end of the question. *Already* is usually stressed to show surprise.

Have you already finished your science project?

We form the present perfect with the verb *have* and the past participle of the main verb. For a full list of irregular verbs, See page 175.

▶ 7.2	I / you / we / they	he / she / it
+	We've **already heard** the news.	The bus **has already left** the station.
–	They **haven't found** the keys **yet**.	He **hasn't paid** the bill **yet**.
?	**Have** you **been** to the mall **yet**?	**Has** she **spoken** to the police **yet**?
Y/N	Yes, I **have**. / No, I **haven't**. / **Not yet**.	Yes, she **has**. / No, she **hasn't**. / **Not yet**.

> **Look!** In American English we can also use *yet* and *already* with the simple past:
> *We already gave him the papers.*
> *The supermarket didn't open yet.*
> *Did Helen already call you?*

1 Complete the conversation with the words in the box.

> already   yet

A Watching TV again? What about your homework?
B I've [1]_____ done it.
A When did you do it?
B On the bus from school ... so now I'm watching the game.
A The game? Has it started [2]_____?
B Yes! It just started, so you haven't missed anything [3]_____.
A Great! Let me sit down. I want to watch this, too!

2 Choose the correct words to complete the sentences.

1 **A** I have to clean the kitchen tonight.
   B Don't worry. I've *yet / already* cleaned it this week.
2 **A** Has Flora passed her driving test *yet / already*?
   B Yes, and she only took five lessons!
3 **A** Can I speak to Julia, please?
   B She was here a minute ago, but I think she's *yet / already* left the office.
4 Teresa hasn't booked her flight *yet / already*. It will be very expensive!
5 **A** Should we watch *Titanic* tonight?
   B Do we have to? I've *yet / already* seen it about twenty times!
6 Have you used the new bike lane *yet / already*? It's much safer.
7 **A** I think we need to fill up the tank with gas.
   B It's OK. I've *yet / already* been to the gas station today.
8 He only joined the company a year ago, and they've *just / yet / already* promoted him twice!

3 Make sentences using *yet,* or *already*.

1 she / not pack / her suitcase (yet)
   _____

2 I / send you / a wedding invitation (already)
   _____

3 the game / start (already)
   _____

4 you / speak / to Charles? (yet)
   _____

5 I / can't buy / a new apartment (yet)
   _____

6 I / have / three cups of coffee today (already)
   _____

124   ◀ Go back to page 59

7C Present perfect with *for* and *since*

We use the present perfect with *for* and *since* to talk about a situation that started in the past and is still true now.

How long have you lived in Brazil? NOT *How long are you living in Brazil?*
I've lived here all my life. NOT *I'm living here all my life.*

We use *since* to refer to a fixed point in time in the past when the situation started.

I've worked for this company since 2010.
I haven't spoken to Fred since last summer.
Have you known Mark since you were a child?

We use *for* to refer to the period of time the situation has been true.

Joseph has been a teacher for two months.
This computer hasn't worked for years!
Has the building been here for a long time?

We use *How long …?* to ask about the length of time a situation has been true.

How long have you known your boyfriend?
We've known each other since last March.
How long has he been a doctor?
He's been a doctor for about two years.

We form the present perfect with the verb *have* and the past participle of the main verb. For a complete list of irregular verbs, see page 175.

▶ 7.12

	I / you / we / they	he / she / it
+	I**'ve lived** in this part of the city **for** two years. They**'ve worked** together **since** 1990.	Sam**'s had** this car **for** over 20 years. It**'s been** much hotter **since** last weekend.
−	We **haven't spoken** to each other **for** a year. I **haven't gone** swimming in the ocean **since** I was a child.	Isabella **hasn't worn** her glasses **for** a long time. He **hasn't driven** a car **since** he had the accident.
?	**How long have** you **known** her?	**How long has** he **been** a teacher?

Present perfect or simple past

We use the simple past to talk about completed actions in the past. We can often give the same information in two different ways.

a period of time / an unfinished action	a point in the past / a completed action
I've lived in Uruguay for ten years.	I moved to Uruguay ten years ago.
Jo has known me since I was 16 years old.	Jo met me when I was 16 years old.
How long have you worked here?	When did you start working here?
I haven't eaten meat since 2010.	I gave up meat in 2010.

We use the simple past to talk about a time period that started and finished in the past.

How long did you live in Bolivia?
I lived there for ten years.
I lived there from 1980 to 1990.
= I don't live there now.

How long have you lived in Chile?
I've lived here for almost ten years.
I've lived here since 2010.
= I live here now.

1 Put the times in the box in the correct column: *for* or *since*.

> 1997   9:30 a.m.   a couple of hours   a few seconds
> a long time   ages   April   five months
> he was a child   I finished college   last night
> most of my life   my accident   seventeen years
> several weeks   the middle of June   the weekend
> three centuries   Thursday

for	since

2 Write sentences using the present perfect form of the verbs in parentheses. Write one sentence with *for* and one with *since*.

1 I moved to Istanbul in the middle of July. It's the middle of December now. (live)
   I've lived in Istanbul for five months.
   I've lived in Istanbul since the middle of July.
2 I bought my own car when I was 19. I'm 23 now. (have)
   _____
   _____
3 The last time I was on an airplane was in August. That was six months ago. (not be)
   _____
   _____
4 I met my best friend when I was five. I'm 22 now. (know)
   _____
   _____
5 I gave up English in 2005. That was ages ago. (not study)
   _____
   _____

3 Choose the correct form of the verbs to complete the sentences.

1 He *didn't speak / hasn't spoken* to his mom since he *got back / 's gotten back* from his vacation.
2 I *bought / 've bought* this car in 2007, so I *'m having / 've had* it for more than ten years now.
3 I'm a sales manager and I *worked / 've worked* in this department for two years. Before that, I *worked / 've worked* in marketing from 2012 to 2015.
4 We *knew / 've known* each other for about ten years, in fact, since we *met / 've met* in college.
5 I *was / 've been* worried about Frank since he *lost / 's lost* his job.
6 He *lost / 's lost* his phone this morning, so I *'m not speaking / haven't spoken* to him for a few hours now.
7 I *lived / 've lived* in Chicago for two years, but then I *moved / 've moved* to Washington D.C., and I *lived / 've lived* here since then.
8 Their wedding *was / has been* in May, so they *are / 've been* married for nearly six months now.

◀ Go back to page 62

GRAMMAR PRACTICE

8A too, too many, too much, and (not) enough

We use *too, too many,* and *too much* to mean "more than necessary" or "more than is good."

This exam is too difficult. There are too many questions!

We use *too* before adjectives and adverbs.

That restaurant is too expensive.
She works too hard.

We use *too many* before countable nouns.

I drink too many cups of coffee.

We use *too much* before uncountable nouns.

I eat too much chocolate.

We can also use *too much* after a verb without an object.

He worries too much.

We use *enough* to mean "the right amount" or "sufficient." We can also use *not enough* to mean "less than necessary" or "less than is good."

Is your coffee sweet enough? I didn't have enough sugar for everyone.

Enough comes before countable and uncountable nouns.

He doesn't eat enough vegetables.
Have we got enough time?

Enough comes after an adjective or adverb.

The information isn't clear enough.
He didn't sing well enough to win the competition.

We can also use *enough* after a verb without an object.

I didn't sleep enough last night.

▶ 8.2	too / too many / too much	(not) enough
Countable nouns	You shouldn't watch **too many movies**.	We have **enough eggs** to bake two cakes.
Uncountable nouns	Jen drinks **too much coffee** in the morning.	Do you have **enough money** to buy those shoes?
Adjectives	The train is **too crowded** at rush hour.	The soup is**n't hot enough**.

1 Choose the correct words to complete the sentences.

1 She eats *too much / too many* candy.
2 They don't eat *enough vegetables / vegetables enough.*
3 Our apartment is *too much / too* small for a party.
4 He puts *too much / too many* sugar in his coffee.
5 Are you sure you're *well enough / enough well* to run a marathon?
6 You eat *too much / too many* junk food.
7 I don't have *enough money / money enough* to buy a new car.
8 These jeans are *too much / too* big for me now that I've lost weight.

2 Complete the sentences using *too, too many, too much,* and *enough.*

1 You eat _____ takeout meals. Don't you ever cook?
2 Don't cook the broccoli for _____ long.
3 My English isn't good _____ to have a conversation.
4 You drink _____ coffee. It isn't good for you.
5 I don't earn _____ money to buy a house.
6 I'm _____ tired to go out tonight.
7 My son spends _____ time playing computer games.
8 I have a stomachache. I ate _____ cupcakes.

3 Rewrite the sentences using the words in parentheses.

1 You should get more exercise. (enough)
   You don't get enough exercise.
2 You eat more sugar than you should. (much)
   _____
3 She's too young to drive. (old)
   _____
4 It isn't quiet enough to work. (noisy)
   _____
5 We need more gasoline. (enough)
   _____
6 There are more cars on the road than there should be. (too)
   _____

◀ Go back to page 67

GRAMMAR PRACTICE

8C have to, not have to, and can't

We use *have to* to talk about obligations and rules.
You always **have to lock** the door when you leave.
Amy **has to wear** formal clothes to work.

When we ask questions about obligations and rules, we usually use *have to*.
Do you **have to start** work early?
Why **do** we **have to park** the car here?

We use *don't have to* to say that something isn't necessary.
You **don't have to speak** English for this job, but it's useful.
Kasim **doesn't have to work** today. It's a holiday in Hong Kong.

We use *can't* to talk about things that are not allowed. We call this prohibition.
I **can't eat** any potato chips. I'm on a diet.
You **can't start** the exam until I say.

▶ 8.9

	I / you / we / they	he / she / it
have to	I **have to work** late again tonight, unfortunately. Do you **have to take** the bus today? Yes, I **do**. / No, I **don't**.	Jackie **has to study** math in school. Does he **have to wait** a long time? Yes, he **does**. / No, he **doesn't**.
not have to	You **don't have to pay**–it's free!	He **doesn't have to wear** a uniform to school.
can't	I **can't be** late for the meeting.	Luke **can't eat** too much salt.

Look! Remember, *can't* and *don't have to* have different meanings.
You **can't walk** on the grass. = It's not allowed.
You **don't have to walk** on the grass—you can walk on the path. = it's not necessary. You can choose.

---

1 Make sentences using the positive (+), negative (–), or question form (?) of *have to*.

1 What time / you / arrive / at the airport (?)
   _____
2 My sister / study / English / in school (+)
   _____
3 You / show / your passport / to enter the country (–)
   _____
4 Lenny / cook / dinner / tonight (?)
   _____
5 We / finish / the project / until next week (–)
   _____
6 You / drive / on the left / in the U.K. (+)
   _____

2 Choose the correct words to complete the conversation.

   A What's wrong, David?
   B My brother ¹*can't / has to* go to the hospital tomorrow.
   A Oh no! Why does he ²*can't / have to* go?
   B It's nothing serious. He ³*has to / can't* have a blood test.
   A Does he ⁴*have to / has to* spend the night there?
   B No, he ⁵*hasn't / doesn't*. The worst thing is he ⁶*doesn't have to / can't* eat anything for 24 hours.
   A I ⁷*don't have to / can't* work tomorrow. I can give him a ride to the hospital, if you want.
   B Thanks, Ada. That's great. He ⁸*has to / can't* be there at 10:00 a.m.
   A That's fine.
   B Great, he'll be happy he ⁹*can't / doesn't have to* take the bus ... especially without any breakfast!

3 Look at the poster. Complete the rules for the swimming pool with the verbs in parentheses.

1 Adults _____ (pay) to use the pool.
2 Children _____ (pay) to go swimming.
3 You _____ (eat) by the pool.
4 You _____ (take) a shower before you swim.
5 You _____ (run) near the pool.

◀ Go back to page 71

GRAMMAR PRACTICE

9A *used to*

We use *used to* + the base form to talk about habits or situations that were true in the past, but aren't true now.

I used to ride my bike to school every day. = I don't ride my bike to school now.
I used to live in a small town. = I don't live there now.

We form the negative with *didn't* + *use to* + the base form.

I didn't use to drink so much coffee. (= I drink a lot now).
She didn't use to like spicy food. (= She likes it a lot now).

We form questions with *did* + *use to* + the base form.

Did you use to play on the school basketball team?
Why did you use to have two cars?

We can use the simple past instead of *used to*. The meaning is the same.

I used to have English classes at school = I had English classes at school.
She used to be shy when she was younger = She was shy when she was younger.

We don't use *used to* to talk about actions that only happened once.

I bought this shirt last year. NOT ~~I used to buy this shirt last year.~~
They started work at 9:00 this morning. NOT ~~They used to start work at 9:00 this morning.~~

▶ 9.1	I / you / he / she / it / we / they
+	I **used to like** reggae music when I was younger.
–	He **didn't use to be** as rich as he is now.
?	**Did** you **use to go** to the beach every day when you lived in Acapulco?
Y/N	Yes, I **did**. / No, I **didn't**.

> **Look!** *Used to* only refers to the past. We use *usually* + simple present to talk about habits and situations that are true now.
> *Harry usually takes the bus to work.*
> *He's not usually late for class.*
> *How do you usually contact your family?*

1 Read the text. Write sentences with *used to* or *didn't use to* and the verbs in parentheses.

> ### He used to be rich!
> George Kaltsidis lives in a small house in the north of England. He drives an old Ford Fiesta and wears a secondhand watch. However, believe it or not, George used to be a millionaire and lived a life of luxury. He wasn't happy, and last year he gave all his money away to charity. He's much happier now, he says. But what did his life use to be like?

1 He (live) in a small house. He (live) in an expensive apartment.
He didn't use to live in a small house. He used to live in an expensive apartment.

2 He (drive) an old car. He (have) a new BMW.
_____

3 He (be) very lonely because he (see) his family or friends very much.
_____

4 He (wear) expensive clothes and he never (buy) secondhand things.
_____

5 He (go) on luxury vacations, but he (enjoy) himself.
_____

2 Complete the sentences with the positive, negative, or question form of *used to* and the verbs in the box.

> have (x2)   play   work   argue   go   like   be

1 They _____ a house in Spain, but they sold it last year.

2 _____ you _____ a lot of sports when you were younger?

3 I _____ to the gym, but now I usually go three times a week.

4 _____ you _____ with your parents a lot?

5 Where _____ you _____ before you got this job?

6 She _____ long hair, but now she prefers it short.

7 I _____ fish, but I love it now.

8 There _____ a park here before they built those office buildings.

3 Complete the sentences with *used to* or the simple past form of the verbs in parentheses if *used to* is not possible.

1 Did you _____ a school uniform? (wear)

2 I _____ my arm when I was eight. I was ten. (not break)

3 I _____ badly behaved in school. (be)

4 My parents _____ a lot of money. (not earn)

5 I _____ a $50 bill on the sidewalk one day. (find)

6 My grandma _____ listening to the radio. (love)

7 I _____ a lot of computer games when I was a teenager. (play)

8 The first movie I _____ at a theater was *Titanic*. (see)

128

◀ Go back to page 77

GRAMMAR PRACTICE

9C The passive

Sentences can be either active or passive.
Active: *My brother wrote this book.*
Passive: *This book was written by my brother.*
We use the active sentence to focus on the person who does the action.
My brother wrote this book.
We use the passive sentence to focus on the action itself or on the thing the action affects.
This book was written by my brother.
We also use the passive when we don't know who does/did the action or it isn't important.
These coffeemakers are made in Italy.
My wallet was stolen yesterday.
We form the simple present passive with *am/is/are* + past participle of the main verb.
We form the simple past passive with *was/were* + past participle of the main verb.
Simple present passive: *Toyota cars are built in Japan.*
Simple past passive: *The buildings were destroyed five years ago.*
To say who does/did the action, we use *by*.
Lots of hotel towels are taken by tourists as souvenirs.
This building was designed in 1985, by a Chinese architect.
To form questions, we put the verb *be* before the subject.
Is your watch made of gold?
When was the book written?
Who was the music sung by?

▶ 9.12	Simple present passive	Simple past passive
+	The soccer games **are played** in the evening.	The movie **was directed** by Steven Spielberg.
–	The painting **isn't signed** by the artist.	Chess **wasn't invented** in Europe.
?	**Are** these cookies **made** with butter?	**Were** the workers **paid** last month?
Y/N	**Yes**, they **are**. / **No**, they **aren't**.	**Yes**, they **were**. / **No**, they **weren't**.

1 Write sentences in the simple present or past passive.
 1 English / speak / here (simple present)
  English is spoken here.
 2 This guitar / play / by Jimi Hendrix (simple past)
  _____
 3 The soup / make / with fresh vegetables (simple present)
  _____
 4 When / the photos / take? (simple past)
  _____
 5 Who / the movie / direct / by? (simple past)
  _____
 6 Credit cards / not accept / here (simple present)
  _____

2 Rewrite the sentences in the passive.
 1 More than 162 million people use eBay.
  eBay _____ .
 2 The Channel Tunnel connects Britain and France.
  Britain and France _____ .
 3 Facebook bought WhatsApp for $22 billion.
  WhatsApp _____ .
 4 Steven Spielberg didn't direct *Jurassic World*.
  Jurassic World _____ .
 5 They make sushi with rice and raw fish.
  Sushi _____ .
 6 Did Tolstoy write *War and Peace*?
  Was _____ .

3 Complete the text with the active or passive form of the verbs in parentheses.

HIDDEN TREASURE

Treasure Detectives is a British TV show and it [1]____ (watch) by more than 300,000 viewers. Each week, two different objects [2]____ (examine) very carefully by experts to find out if they are valuable treasures or copies of original works.

Robert Darvell [3]____ (contact) the show and [4]____ (ask) them to help him find out more about a painting he had. Robert's father [5]____ (buy) a box of objects, which included a small painting, for £30 at an auction in 2003. The painting [6]____ (keep) in a drawer for many years and eventually it [7]____ (give) to Robert.

After almost a year, Robert [8]____ (tell) the truth about the painting on live TV. The experts [9]____ (say) it was by the English artist, John Constable, and it was worth about £250,000! He was surprised, but very happy.

◀ Go back to page 80

GRAMMAR PRACTICE

10A Past perfect

We use the past perfect to describe an action that happened before another action in the past.

I arrived at the meeting late because I'd missed the train.
Justine hadn't studied for the exam, so she failed it.
Had you met Sergio before you started the job?

We form the past perfect with *had* + the past participle of the main verb.

▶ 10.5 Past perfect

+	He**'d forgotten** his wallet, so he couldn't buy anything.
−	We **hadn't tried** ceviche before we visited Peru.
?	**Had** you **trained** a lot before you ran the marathon?
Y/N	Yes, I **had**. / No, I **hadn't**.

Look! The contracted form of the past perfect is the same as the contracted form of *would*.
I'd seen him before. = *I had seen him before.*
I'd see him if I could. = *I would see him if I could.*

Narrative tenses

We usually use the past perfect with the simple past and the past continuous to show when actions happened.

When I got home, my husband cooked the dinner.

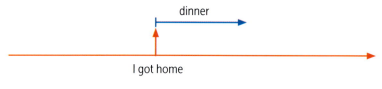

When I got home, my husband was cooking dinner.

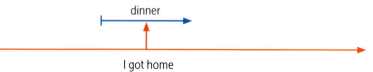

When I got home, my husband had cooked dinner.

1 Match the two parts to make sentences.

1 Sofia had seen the movie before _____
2 Jeff felt very bad because _____
3 Susana hadn't had lunch, so _____
4 Paul had grown a beard, so _____
5 When I got to the station, _____
6 Anna had finished the report when _____

a I got to work this morning.
b she felt very hungry.
c and she said it wasn't very good.
d the bus had already left.
e I didn't recognize him.
f he'd forgotten his niece's birthday.

2 Complete the conversations with the past perfect form of the verbs in parentheses.

1 **A** Why did they walk to college today?
   B They _____ (have) a problem with the car.
2 **A** _____ you _____ (hear) about the problems at the airport before you left?
   B No, I hadn't. Luckily, they _____ (not make) any changes to my flight.
3 **A** Rita bought me a book for my birthday, but I _____ (read) it before.
   B It's my fault. She bought it because I _____ (recommend) it to her.
4 **A** Was Grandma pleased that the kids _____ (draw) a picture for her?
   B Yes, she was. They _____ (not do) one for her before.
5 **A** _____ Ricky _____ (look) everywhere before he canceled his credit card?
   B No, he _____ (not look) in his sports bag. He found it there this morning.

3 Complete the text with the simple past, past continuous, or past perfect form of the verbs in parentheses.

On April 21, 1980, Rosie Ruiz ¹_____ (cross) the finish line of the Boston Marathon with a time of 2:31:56–the fastest female time in Boston Marathon history. However, when she ²_____ (receive) the winner's medal, some judges ³_____ (become) suspicious because she ⁴_____ (not sweat) very much. Then two students ⁵_____ (say) that they ⁶_____ (see) her join the race half a mile from the finish line. Later, photographer Susan Morrow said she ⁷_____ (meet) Ruiz while she ⁸_____ (ride) on the subway in her running clothes at the time of the New York marthon, six months earlier. The judges ⁹_____ (discover) that Ruiz ¹⁰_____ (do) the same thing to win the Boston Marathon.

◀ Go back to page 85

10C Reported speech

When someone speaks, we call what they say "direct speech." When we talk about what they said afterward, we call it "reported speech."

"I don't like the website." ⇒ My boss said that he didn't like the website.
"We reserved a room." ⇒ They told me that they had reserved a room.

We use the verbs *say* and *tell* to report speech. We use *tell* with a noun or a pronoun when we want to say who the person was speaking to. We can add *that* to reported speech sentences.

"I'm sorry." ⇒ He said (that) he was sorry.
⇒ He told me (that) he was sorry.

The tense of the verb usually changes when we report speech.

Direct speech		Reported speech
simple present	⇒	simple past
present continuous	⇒	past continuous
simple past	⇒	past perfect
present perfect	⇒	past perfect
past perfect	⇒	past perfect
am/is/are going to	⇒	was/were going to
will	⇒	would
can	⇒	could

Look! We also change pronouns and possessive adjectives in reported speech.
"I sold my car to Lenny." ⇒ He said that he'd sold his car to Lenny.
"We'll send you the letter." ⇒ They said they'd send me the letter.

▶ 10.12

	Direct speech		Reported speech
simple present	"I drink too much coffee."	⇒	She told me she drank too much coffee.
present continuous	"We're studying for the exam."	⇒	They said they were studying for the exam.
simple past	"Karl didn't go to the store."	⇒	She said Karl hadn't gone to the store.
present perfect	"I haven't been to Paris."	⇒	He said he hadn't been to Paris.
past perfect	"We'd seen the movie before."	⇒	They said they'd seen the movie before.
going to	"Michelle is going to drive home."	⇒	He said Michelle was going to drive home.
will	"I'll open the letter."	⇒	He told me he'd open the letter.
can	"Ruby can't swim."	⇒	They told him Ruby couldn't swim.

1 Choose the correct words to complete the sentences.
   1 My teacher *said / told* me that my English was improving.
   2 The doctor *said / told* you had to stay in bed.
   3 Victor *said / told* he had made a big mistake.
   4 Someone *said / told* us that you had started a blog.
   5 They *said / told* everyone they would win the game.
   6 The newsreader *said / told* that scientists had discovered a new planet.

2 Rewrite these sentences in reported speech.
   1 "I'll see you on Tuesday."
     My mom told me _____.
   2 "It's not going to rain this week."
     The weather forecaster said _____.
   3 "I've never eaten curry."
     Julieta said _____.
   4 "We saw your brother at the airport."
     They told me _____.
   5 "I hadn't heard the news."
     Bobby said _____.
   6 "I can't come to your wedding."
     Ravi told me _____.
   7 "I'm waiting for a phone call."
     My boss said _____.
   8 "I don't get much exercise."
     Sandra said _____.

3 Write the direct speech for the reported sentences.

   1 Sheila and Harold said that they wanted to tell me their news.
     _____
   2 They told me that they'd been on vacation to Egypt.
     _____
   3 They said they'd been excited because they'd never been there before.
     _____
   4 Sheila said that she'd never ride a camel again.
     _____
   5 Harold told me he was going to go back next year.
     _____

◀ Go back to page 89

131

GRAMMAR PRACTICE

11A *-ing* and infinitive verb patterns

We often use two verbs together. The form of the second verb changes depending on the first verb.

I want to learn a new language.
I enjoy learning new languages.

After some verbs, we use the infinitive.

▶ 11.2	infinitive
decide	She decided to travel the world.
arrange	We've arranged to meet at the airport.
expect	I expect to have the results next week.
forget	Marcus forgot to buy any paper for the printer.
hope	He hopes to be here soon.
agree	They haven't agreed to lower the price.
can afford	He can't afford to go on vacation.
manage	The driver managed to stop the train.
learn	I'm learning to speak Italian.
offer	They offered to pay for the meal.
plan	We're planning to open a new office.
try	Patricia's trying to finish the project on time.
want	My sister wants to find a new job.
would like	I'd like to take a break now.
promise	Saul promised to help me with the work.

After other verbs, we use the *-ing* form.

▶ 11.3	*-ing* form
imagine	Can you imagine living until you're 150?
feel like	I feel like staying in bed all day.
enjoy	My son enjoys visiting his grandparents.
suggest	They've suggested installing some new software.
spend (time)	I spend a lot of time getting to work.
miss	She misses seeing her friends.
finish	Tony's finished building the wall.
hate	I hate being late.
keep	Jorge keeps making mistakes.
like	He doesn't like cooking dinner.
love	I love playing golf.
can't stand	Ramon can't stand sleeping in a tent.
mind	They don't mind getting up early.
look forward to	I'm looking forward to seeing you at the party.

Look! After some verbs, we can use the infinitive or the *-ing* form, with no difference in meaning, e.g., *start* and *continue*.
It has started to rain.   *It has started raining.*
He continued to study.   *He continued studying.*

1 Choose the correct form of the verbs to complete the sentences.

1 Have you finished *to clean* / *cleaning* the kitchen?
2 Josh arranged *to meet* / *meeting* Natasha at the theater.
3 She promised *to do* / *doing* her homework.
4 I don't mind *to wait* / *waiting* for you.
5 They agreed *to fix* / *fixing* my dishwasher.
6 You should learn *to use* / *using* the computer.
7 We didn't expect *to see* / *seeing* them again.
8 He spent the whole morning *to sunbathe* / *sunbathing*.
9 Our teacher keeps *to give* / *giving* us lots of homework.
10 She offered *to help* / *helping me* with my English.
11 David suggested *to cancel* / *canceling* the meeting.
12 Don't forget *to bring* / *bringing* warm clothes.

2 Complete the conversation with the correct form of the verbs in parentheses.

Julia Felipe and I have decided [1]_____ (move) back to Brazil.

Sophie Really? I thought you liked [2]_____ (live) in France.

Julia Yes, but we miss [3]_____ (see) our families and we'd like [4]_____ (have) our own house. We could never afford [5]_____ (buy) a place in Paris.

Sophie When are you planning [6]_____ (leave)?

Julia Well, we don't want [7]_____ (wait) too long, so we expect [8]_____ (go) some time in the next couple of months. I've already managed [9]_____ (find) a job, and Felipe is hoping [10]_____ (get) one soon.

Sophie It won't be the same here without you. Do you promise [11]_____ (stay) in touch?

Julia Yes, of course. And if you and Dan feel like [12]_____ (come) to Brazil on vacation, you'd be very welcome at our home in Rio.

Sophie That sounds great. Don't forget [13]_____ (give) me your e-mail address before you go.

Julia Don't worry, I won't. We're trying [14]_____ (plan) a party before we go so that we can say goodbye to everyone. Do you want [15]_____ (come)?

Sophie I hate [16]_____ (say) goodbye to people, but yes, I'd love to come!

132

◀ Go back to page 95

11C Articles

We use articles (*a*, *an*, or *the*) before nouns. Sometimes we don't need to use an article.

▶ 11.13	articles
Indefinite article *a/an*	I have **a** pet dog and **a** pet cat.
Definite article *the*	**The** dog is much bigger than **the** cat.
No article	I love animals, especially dogs and cats.

We use the indefinite article *a/an*:

- to talk about a person or thing for the first time.
  I have two children—a boy and a girl.
- to talk about a person's job.
  My sister's an engineer.
- in expressions of frequency or measurement.
  I see him once a week.
  The fish costs $10 a kg.

We use the definite article *the*:

- if we have already mentioned the person or thing, or we know which one is referred to.
  The boy is named Alex, and the girl is named Lucy.
- if there is only one of the thing.
  The sun is setting.
  I'll check on the Internet.
- before some countries, especially if they have two words or are plural.
  I live in the U.S., but my brother lives in the Philippines.
- for specific places in a town.
  I went to the bank / the movie theater / the grocery store.
- for musical instruments.
  She plays the guitar.
- for superlatives.
  He's the fastest runner in the world.

We don't use an article:

- to talk about things in general (plural and uncountable nouns).
  Dogs are my favorite animals.
  Pollution is a big problem today.
- for some places we visit regularly.
  I'm not going to work today.
  He's working at home.
  She had to go to college.
- for meals, days of the week, months, and years.
  On Tuesday, I'm having lunch with Jack.
  August is my favourite month.

1 Complete the sentences with *a/an*, *the*, or – (no article).

 1 We usually go to ____ movies once or twice ____ month.
 2 I bought ____ new car yesterday, but this morning ____ engine won't start.
 3 He's one of five brothers. ____ youngest brother is ____ doctor.
 4 She flew from ____ Venezuela to ____ U.S.
 5 Are you really scared of ____ spiders?
 6 How long have you played ____ piano?
 7 Neil Armstrong was ____ first man on ____ moon.
 8 I hope you both find ____ happiness together.
 9 What did you have for ____ breakfast this morning?
 10 We have ____ dinner together three times ____ year.
 11 She got ____ home from ____ work and went straight to ____ bed.
 12 ____ Friday is ____ busiest day of ____ week for us.

2 Correct the mistakes or check (✓) the sentences if they are already correct.

 1 Is she student?
 2 I'm staying in bed this morning.
 3 Why don't you ask her out for lunch?
 4 Excuse me, where is museum?
 5 It's beautiful day today.
 6 The life is hard sometimes.
 7 Our taxi driver was from Mexico.
 8 I went to bank this morning.
 9 My wife has never liked tomatoes.
 10 It's best present I've ever received.

3 Complete the text with *a/an*, *the*, or – (no article).

Hexoskin is [1]____ Canadian company founded in [2]____ 2006. It wanted to create [3]____ clothes that could record [4]____ information about our bodies. That's why they developed [5]____ smart shirt that contains lots of sensors. [6]____ sensors collect data about the wearer's movements, heart rate, and breathing and send it to [7]____ computer. Ariane Lavigne is [8]____ Olympic athlete who uses it, and she says [9]____ technology gives her [10]____ advantage over other snowboarders.

◀ Go back to page 99

GRAMMAR PRACTICE

12A Defining relative clauses

We use relative clauses to say which person, thing, or place we are talking about.

He's the actor who was Sherlock Holmes on TV.
It's a machine that bakes bread.
That's the restaurant where I used to work.

We use the relative pronouns *who* or *that* to talk about people.

The man who sits next to me at work was sick today.
I saw the woman that works at the post office in the park.

We use the relative pronouns *that* to talk about things.

There are companies that plan weddings for people.
Louise enjoys movies that make her laugh.

In some cases it is possible to omit *that* entirely.

This is the sweater (that) he gave me for my birthday.

We use *where* to talk about places.

I want to visit the stadium where our team plays soccer.
Jorge works in the hospital where I was born.

▶ 12.2	**defining relative clauses**
To describe people	He's the teacher **who** taught me English. Did you see the children **that** were singing?
To describe things	That's the dog **that** bit me on the leg. I bought the flowers **(that)** she likes.
To describe places	I'll meet you in the square **where** we met last time.

> **Look!** *Who*, *that*, and *where* refer to a person, thing, or place that's already
> been mentioned so we don't need to use another word again.
> *Snakes are the animals that ~~they~~ kill most people each year.*
> *I'd prefer to see the doctor who ~~she~~ saw me last time.*
> *Ronald went to the movie theater where we saw the Star Wars movie ~~there~~.*

1 Complete the sentences with *who*, *that*, or *where*.

1 She opened the box _____ arrived this morning.
2 This is the nightclub _____ Nicola met her boyfriend.
3 There's a meeting at 2:00 p.m. for all employees _____ work in the sales department.
4 The office _____ she spends most of her time is in Kuala Lumpur.
5 The person _____ started this company is now a millionaire.
6 My father-in-law doesn't like movies _____ are too violent.

2 Add the correct words: *who*, *that*, or *where*. Then match the two parts to make sentences.

1 An umbrella is something ____*that*____   ___f___
2 A DJ is someone _____   _____
3 A hospital is a place _____   _____
4 A credit card is something _____   _____
5 An enemy is a person _____   _____
6 A passport is a document _____   _____
7 A department store is somewhere _____   _____
8 A selfie stick is something _____   _____
9 A single parent is someone _____   _____
10 A prison is a place _____   _____

a you go when you're sick.
b you use when you travel abroad.
c you use to take a photo of yourself.
d brings up a child without a partner.
e criminals are sent.
f ~~you use when it rains.~~
g plays music in a club or on the radio.
h you can buy lots of different things.
i someone hates.
j you use instead of cash to buy things.

3 Combine the pairs of sentences using *who*, *where*, *that*, or no relative pronoun. Remember not to use words that aren't necessary.

1 That's the restaurant. We're going there tonight.
   That's the restaurant where we're going tonight.
2 I know the man. He lives in that house.

   _____
3 Did you enjoy the movie? You watched it last night.

   _____
4 They're the neighbors. They have lots of parties.

   _____
5 We've reserved a room in the hotel. We stayed there last summer.

   _____
6 My sister-in-law works for a company. It develops apps.

   _____

◀ Go back to page 103

12C Uses of the -ing form and the infinitive

We use the *-ing* form after prepositions. In the negative, *not* goes before the *-ing* form.

Thanks for inviting me to your wedding.
I'm bored with not going out.
He's worried about failing his exam.

We also use the *-ing* form as the subject or object of a sentence. The *-ing* form functions as a noun.

Keeping in touch is so easy these days.
Reading is a great way to improve your English.
Not drinking soft drinks has helped me to lose weight.
John doesn't enjoy reading.
I love dancing.

We use the infinitive after adjectives. In the negative, *not* goes before the *to*.

I'm amazed to hear that they're going out with each other.
She was disappointed to lose the tennis match.
It's impossible not to laugh when you watch this movie.

We also use the infinitive to say why we do something (to express the purpose).

I went shopping to buy a new pair of shoes.
She left the office to meet a friend.
They're saving all of their money to get married.

> **Look!** We use *for* + *-ing* form to explain the function of things, but we use the infinitive to explain the purpose of actions.
> **Function:** This button is for turning up the volume.
> **Purpose:** You press this button to turn up the volume.

▶ 12.6 -ing form/infinitive

After prepositions	I'm interested **in buying** a new laptop.
As subject/object of a sentence	**Riding** a bike is a great way to stay in shape. I love **riding** my bike.
After adjectives	It's **easy to forget** he's only eighteen.
To express a purpose	We have to leave soon **to get there on time**.

GRAMMAR PRACTICE

1 Choose the correct words to complete the sentences.
1 Before *to say* / *saying* anything, please just listen to me.
2 She wants a better job *to earn* / *for earning* more money.
3 He's afraid of *to disappoint* / *disappointing* his father.
4 *To share* / *Sharing* photos is easy with Instagram.
5 I'm really sorry for *to miss* / *missing* your party.
6 I'm delighted *to tell* / *telling* you that we're getting married.
7 *To speak* / *Speaking* another language is really useful in business.
8 She's pleased *not to work* / *not working* for that company.
9 He asked me *to take care of* / *taking care of* his plants.
10 We thought about *not to go* / *not going* to the wedding.

2 Write sentences in the present tense using the *-ing* form or the infinitive.
1 Drink / too much coffee / not be / good for you
   Drinking too much coffee isn't good for you.
2 She really / enjoy / go to the movies
   _____
3 It / not be / expensive / eat / here
   _____
4 She / not be / afraid of / make mistakes
   _____
5 Cook / with friends / be / a nice way to relax
   _____
6 We / delighted / hear your news
   _____
7 He / not be / very good at / stay in touch
   _____
8 I / go / to the gym / stay in shape
   _____

3 Complete the text with the correct form of the verbs in the box.

| be   work   study   get   act |

¹____ happily married for over 50 years isn't easy, but that's what Paul Newman and Joanne Woodward were. In 1950, Paul was working for his family's business, but he was more interested in ²____ , so at the age of 25, he went to Yale University ³____ drama. He was lucky ⁴____ a job as an actor in a play named *Picnic*, where he first met Joanne. After ⁵____ together on the movie *The Long Hot Summer*, they got married. And the rest, as they say, is history.

◀ Go back to page 107   135

VOCABULARY PRACTICE

7A City features

1 ▶ 7.1 Match the words in the box with the pictures 1–14. Listen and check.

| apartment building   crosswalk   streetlight   street sign   sidewalk   bike lane |
| fountain   tunnel   intersection   bridge   bench   trash can   statue   traffic lights |

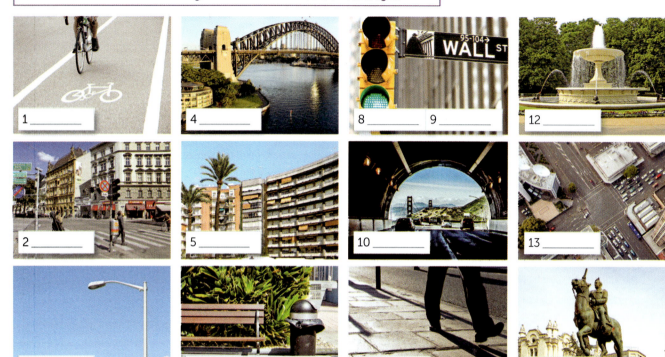

2 Choose the correct options to complete the sentences.

1 The quickest way downtown is to go through the *bridge / tunnel*.
2 He stopped because the *streetlights / traffic light* was red.
3 Use the *crosswalk / trash can*—this street is dangerous.
4 This area is really dirty. I think it's because there aren't any *benches / trash cans*.
5 There's a big *statue / fountain* of a horse in the main square.
6 Follow the *street signs / sidewalk* to get to the national museum.
7 I don't like riding my bike here, there are no *apartment buildings / bike lanes*.
8 Go down this street and turn right at the *intersection / trash cans*.

◀ Go back to page 58

7B Transportation

1 ▶ 7.6 Match the words in the box with the definitions. Listen and check.

| parking lot   commuter   delayed   on time   parking space |
| passenger   platform   public transportation   rush hour   traffic jam |

1 The trains, subways, and buses people use to travel. _____
2 The area in a station where you get on and off a train. _____
3 A person traveling, but not driving. _____
4 Someone who travels to work each day. _____
5 An area or building where people leave their cars. _____
6 The time of day when most people are driving. _____
7 A place where you can leave a single car. _____
8 Slow or late. _____
9 A long line of cars that move very slowly. _____
10 Not early or late. _____

2 ▶ 7.7 Match the sentences. Listen and check.

1 The trains never **arrive on time**. ____
2 It **takes me** nearly two hours to get to work. ____
3 Can I **give you a ride** to the mall? ____
4 I work at a local school, so I usually **walk**. ____
5 I prefer to **ride my bike** into town. ____
6 You need to **start out** earlier. ____
7 It's much quicker to **go by taxi**. ____
8 I have to **take a bus** and **the subway** to work. ____

a I'm going into town anyway.
b That's why I always have my breakfast on the way.
c You'll find one outside the station.
d I usually miss one of them!
e Last week I waited almost 50 minutes on the platform.
f I always talk to people on the way.
g You're always late for work!
h It's faster than walking and there are good bike lanes.

◀ Go back to page 60

148

VOCABULARY PRACTICE

8A Food and drink

1 8.1 Match the words in the box with the pictures 1–20. Listen and check.

| tomato sauce | beef | shrimp | cereal | cucumber | salmon | lettuce | peppers | fruit juice | pineapple |
| strawberry | lamb | tuna | cabbage | coconut | turkey | flour | peach | eggplant | apple pie |

1 _____ 2 _____ 3 _____ 4 _____
5 _____ 6 _____ 7 _____ 8 _____
9 _____ 10 _____ 11 _____ 12 _____
13 _____ 14 _____ 15 _____ 16 _____
17 _____ 18 _____ 19 _____ 20 _____

2 Complete the sentences with the words in the box.

| strawberries tuna cucumber coconut shrimp fruit juice beef lettuce apple pie tomato sauce flour cereal |

1 For breakfast, I usually have a bowl of _____ and a glass of _____.
2 It's easy to bake bread. You just need _____, water, and salt.
3 I'm allergic to seafood, I can't eat _____.
4 The simplest pizza only has _____ and cheese on top.
5 It's difficult to open the shell of a _____, but the milk inside is delicious.
6 My grandmother is going to bake an _____ for dessert tonight.
7 I'm going to make sushi tonight, so I need some rice and _____.
8 She always has a salad with tomatoes, _____, and _____ for lunch.
9 In the summer, I love eating _____ and cream!
10 I ate some amazing _____ steaks in Argentina.

◀ Go back to page 66

149

VOCABULARY PRACTICE

8C Adjectives to describe food

1 ▶ 8.8 Complete the descriptions 1–8 with the words in the box. Listen and check.

| spicy unhealthy tasty raw fresh crunchy salty delicious sour |
| disgusting healthy vegetarian bitter burned creamy sweet |

1 You can't eat that _____ toast. It will taste _____!

2 Sashimi is made with _____ fish. There's not much fat or salt, so it's very _____.

3 I don't eat meat, so I ordered a _____ curry, but it was so _____ I had to drink a lot of water!

4 I know French fries are _____, but mmm! They're very _____!

5 I don't like black coffee—it's too _____. I prefer a _____ hot chocolate.

6 In Morocco, they make tea with _____ mint and lots of sugar, so it's very _____.

7 You can't eat these snacks quietly; they're too _____. They're _____, too, but perfect with a cold drink.

8 Oh no! I can't use this milk, It's a little _____. My cake has to be _____ to win the competition.

2 Choose the correct words to complete the sentences.

1 **A** Do you remember those *tacos* we ate in Mexico that were full of chilli peppers?
  B I'll never forget that. They were so *burned / spicy / crunchy* that I started crying!

2 **A** How often do you go to the supermarket?
  B Hardly ever. I think the market is the best place to buy *fresh / raw / spicy* ingredients.

3 **A** Is something wrong with your cake?
  B Yes, I used too much sugar and now it's too *salty / tasty / sweet*.

4 **A** What's *lassi*?
  B Oh, you'll love it! It's a *disgusting / bitter / creamy* drink from India made with yogurt.

5 **A** I have some lettuce, cucumbers, and red peppers in the refrigerator.
  B Great! Then we can make a nice *crunchy / creamy / salty* salad for lunch.

6 **A** Do you like lemon juice?
  B No, I don't. It's too *spicy / sour / raw* for me.

◀ Go back to page 70

VOCABULARY PRACTICE

9A Money verbs

1 ▶ 9.3 Complete the sentences with the words in the box. Listen and check.

> owe   borrow   can afford   charge   cost   earn   get paid
> be worth   own   pay back   save   spend   waste   lend

1 Excuse me, how much does this necklace _____?
2 In my opinion, soccer clubs _____ too much for tickets.
3 Waiters can _____ a lot of money from tips.
4 Can you _____ me $50 until I get paid next week?
5 He has a rare 1950s Rolex watch. It must _____ a fortune!
6 As well as their apartment in London, they _____ a house in Hollywood.
7 They _____ most of their money on clothes.
8 How much money do you _____ to the bank each month?
9 The car isn't ours yet. We still _____ the bank $5,000.
10 I've left all my money at home. Can I _____ $20, please?
11 Don't _____ your money on lottery tickets—you'll never win!
12 He's trying to _____ for an expensive trip next summer.
13 She's so rich that she _____ to buy anything she wants.
14 We normally _____ on the last day of the month.

2 Choose the correct words to complete the sentences.

1 Oh no, I've forgotten my wallet. Can you *borrow / lend / owe* me some money?
2 I can't go out tonight. I don't *earn / afford / get paid* until next week.
3 Excuse me, how much does this jacket *cost / worth / charge*?
4 I *spend / waste / save* almost half of my money on rent every month.
5 If you give me $200, I'll *borrow / owe / pay back* the money next week.
6 I bought the guitar for $500, but it's now *worth / cost / earn* almost double that.
7 My car is very old, but I can't *spend / afford / own* to buy a new one right now.
8 When I finish college, I will *owe / lend / charge* the bank more than $10,000.
9 I shouldn't go out this month. I need to *charge / earn / save* for a new computer.
10 Why did you *pay back / waste / earn* all your money on these comic books?

◀ Go back to page 77

9B Shopping

1 ▶ 9.5 Choose the correct verbs to complete the sentences. Listen and check.

1 Can I *pay by / pay with* credit card, or do I have to *pay on / pay with* cash?
2 I'd like to *exchange / return* this jacket—it's too big. Can I *exchange / return* it for a smaller one, please?
3 Can I *try on / fit* these shoes, please? I need to know how they *try on / fit* me.
4 You can *deliver / order* furniture online. Then the company will *deliver / order* it to your house.

2 ▶ 9.6 Match the words in the box with the definitions 1–12. Listen and check.

> dressing room   bargain   receipt   discount   sales   cash
> refund   cash register   window shopping   department store
> line   shopping center

1 A product that a store sells at a very good price. _____
2 A piece of paper that shows you have bought something. _____
3 A time when a store sells things at a lower price than usual. _____
4 The place in a store where you can try on clothes. _____
5 A place where people stand to wait for something. _____
6 The place where you pay for things in a store. _____
7 The money that is returned when a product isn't suitable. _____
8 An amount or percentage off the usual price. _____
9 Money in the form of bills and coins. _____
10 Looking at products in stores without buying anything. _____
11 A large store with areas selling different types of products. _____
12 A covered area with different stores. _____

3 Match the two parts to make sentences.

1 I'm going to try on these jeans ____
2 I'm sorry, I can't give you a refund ____
3 You can stand in this line for the cash register ____
4 This morning I went window shopping ____
5 I bought this handbag on sale for $15; ____
6 I bought it at the department store because ____
7 If I pay with cash, ____
8 I ordered these online last week, ____

a can you offer me a discount?
b in the dressing room.
c but you can only pay by credit card.
d it was a real bargain!
e if there's a problem, I can easily return it.
f but I'd like to exchange them for a different color.
g if you don't have the receipt.
h in the shopping mall.

◀ Go back to page 78

151

VOCABULARY PRACTICE

10A Sports and competitions

1 ▶ 10.2 Look at the soccer scores. Complete the text with the verbs in the box in the correct form. Listen and check.

win beat score lose tie

On May 28, 2016, Real Madrid [1]_____ their rivals, Atlético, in the final of the UEFA Champions League. Ramos [2]_____ a goal first, but 65 minutes later, Carrasco managed to score again to [3]_____ the game 1–1. After extra time, Real Madrid was lucky to [4]_____ the game on penalties. Atlético was very disappointed to [5]_____ because in 2014, they had also lost to Real Madrid in the final.

Look! We use *win* for a competition or award, and we use *beat* for another team or opponent.
Real Madrid won the Champions League.
Real Madrid beat Atlético.

2 ▶ 10.3 Match the words in the box with the pictures 1–10. Listen and check.

| athlete crowd player medal race referee
spectator umpire trophy game |
|---|

3 ▶ 10.4 Read sentences. 1–4. Match the verbs in **bold** with definitions a–d. Listen and check.

1 Over 200 countries **take part** in the Olympic Games every four years. ____
2 It's difficult to **cheat** in sports events, but some athletes still try. ____
3 Before you play any sports, you should always **warm up**. ____
4 I couldn't finish the marathon. I had to **give up** after 20 kilometers. ____

a break the rules to try to win a game or pass a test
b stop doing something because it's too difficult
c play in a game or competition
d do special exercises to prepare your body for sports

4 Choose the correct words to complete the sentences.

1 The *referee* / *umpire* showed three soccer players the red card.
2 I was injured because I didn't *give up* / *warm up* before the game.
3 My grandfather won a bronze *medal* / *race* in the Olympic Games.
4 The L.A. Lakers *beat* / *won* the Chicago Bulls by 123 to 118.
5 Serena Williams is a very successful *athlete* / *referee*.
6 Your team *cheated* / *scored*. This competition is for under 16-year-olds, but three of your players are 17 years old.
7 We *tied* / *lost* 0–0. It was a really boring game.
8 My sister was in the stadium, so when I watched the game on TV, I looked for her in the *crowd* / *spectator*.
9 The 100-meter *match* / *race* is my favorite part of the Olympics.
10 I'm terrible at tennis. I *beat* / *lost* my last match 0–6, 0–6, 0–6!

1 _____

2 _____

3 _____

4 _____

5 _____

6 _____

7 _____

8 _____

9 _____

10 _____

◀ Go back to page 84

VOCABULARY PRACTICE

10C Parts of the body

1 ▶ 10.9 Match parts of the body *a–x* with the words *1–24*. Listen and check.

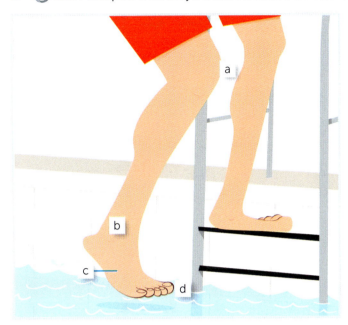

1 foot ____ 2 knee ____ 3 toes ____ 4 ankle ____
5 finger ____ 6 wrist ____ 7 elbow ____ 8 hand ____
9 arm ____ 10 thumb ____

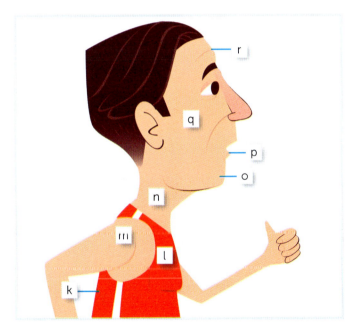

11 neck ____ 12 cheek ____ 13 chest ____ 14 lips ____
15 back ____ 16 chin ____ 17 forehead ____ 18 shoulder ____
19 heart ____ 20 brain ____ 21 stomach ____
22 skin ____ 23 muscle ____ 24 bone ____

2 ~~Cross out~~ the word that is incorrect in each sentence.
  1 I got injured playing football, and now I can't move my *cheeks / elbow / shoulder*.
  2 She can't walk because she's hurt her *ankle / brain / toes*.
  3 I can't write because something is wrong with my *fingers / lips / wrist*.
  4 It was so cold, she was wearing a scarf around her *elbow / neck / shoulders*.
  5 This shirt doesn't fit me because I have a big *chin / neck / chest*.
  6 It's impossible for me to run a marathon because of my bad *ankle / fingers / knee*.
  7 Put this cream on your *lips / muscles / bones* if they hurt.
  8 You need to have a scan at the hospital to be able to see your *bones / heart / forehead* well.
  9 In a warm-up, you have to stretch your *chin / arms / muscles*.

◀ Go back to page 88

153

VOCABULARY PRACTICE

11A Household items

1　11.1 Match the words in the box with the pictures 1–20. Listen and check.

oven sink blanket cushion dishwasher trash can comforter pillow refrigerator iron rug sheets stove faucet air-conditioning washing machine carpet chest of drawers central heating closet

1 _____   2 _____   3 _____   4 _____

5 _____   6 _____   7 _____   8 _____

9 _____   10 _____   11 _____   12 _____

13 _____   14 _____   15 _____   16 _____

17 _____   18 _____   19 _____   20 _____

2　Choose the correct word to complete the sentences.
1　Can you put these glasses in the *trash can / sink*, please? They're dirty.
2　We need new *pillows / cushions* for the sofa. What color would you like?
3　Let's move the *rug / carpet* to the middle of the room.
4　Could you turn on the *air-conditioning / central heating*? It's cold in here.
5　We have a new *dishwasher / washing machine*. My shirts are really clean these days!
6　Help me make the bed. Can you pass me the *sheet / blanket* to put on top?

154　　　　　　　　　　　　　　　　　　　　　　　　　　　　◀ Go back to page 94

VOCABULARY PRACTICE

11B Housework

1 ▶ 11.6 Match the words in the box with the pictures 1–15. Listen and check.

| mop the floor   clear the table   set the table   water the plants   load the dishwasher   do the ironing   vacuum the carpet   wash the dishes |
| sweep the floor   take out the trash   make the bed   dust the furniture   hang out the clothes   do the laundry   put away the toys |

1 _____ 2 _____ 3 _____ 4 _____ 5 _____
6 _____ 7 _____ 8 _____ 9 _____ 10 _____
11 _____ 12 _____ 13 _____ 14 _____ 15 _____

2 Choose the correct word to complete the sentences.

1 The first thing I do every morning is *lay / make / change* my bed.
2 You have to *wash the dishes / do the laundry / hang out the clothes*. The dishwasher is broken.
3 I have lots of allergies, so if I don't *clear / do / dust* the furniture every day, I start to sneeze and cough.
4 These plants will die if you don't *wash / water / clear* them more often.
5 Can you *hang out / take out / water* the clothes, please? They're very wet.
6 My dog leaves hairs on the rug, so I have to *vacuum / mop / clear* it every day.
7 What a wonderful meal! Can you help me *mop / clear / set* the table?
8 My friends are coming over for dinner in twenty minutes, so I need to *clear / make / set* the table.

◀ Go back to page 96

155

VOCABULARY PRACTICE

11C Words to describe materials and clothes

1 ▶ 11.12 Complete the descriptions 1–10 with the words in the box. You will need to use some of the words more than once. Listen and check.

denim   cotton   plastic   leather   silk   fur   wood   glass   wool   metal

1 A _____ shirt. It's made of _____ .

2 A _____ coat. It's made of _____ .

3 Some _____ boots. They're made of _____ .

4 A _____ tie. It's made of _____ .

5 Some _____ shoes. They're made of _____ .

6 A _____ sweater. It's made of _____ .

7 A _____ necklace. It's made of _____ .

8 Some _____ jeans. They're made of _____ .

9 A _____ ring. It's made of _____ .

10 Some _____ beads. They're made of _____ .

2 ▶ 11.13 Match the adjectives with their opposites. Listen and check.

1 plain   ____   a old-fashioned
2 formal   ____   b loose
3 stylish   ____   c striped
4 tight   ____   d casual

3 Look at the pictures. Are the sentences true (T) or false (F)? Correct the false sentences.

1 Helen is wearing a formal jacket. ____
2 She's wearing a silk scarf. ____
3 She's wearing tight pants. ____

4 Joe is wearing casual clothes. ____
5 He's wearing a gray jacket. ____
6 He's wearing a plain tie. ____

7 He has a wood tennis racket. ____
8 He's wearing loose shorts. ____
9 He's wearing a plain T-shirt. ____

◀ Go back to page 98

VOCABULARY PRACTICE

12A Relationships

1 ▶ 12.1 Put the words in the box in the correct columns. Listen and check.

| cousin | only child | roommate | employer | enemy | stranger | twin | ex-husband | stepsister | bride | colleague | neighbor |
| in-laws | boss | girlfriend | groom | single parent | relative | employee | business partner | classmate | brother-in-law |

family	couple	work/study	home	other

2 Complete the sentences with the words from exercise 1.

1. Daisy and I work in the same office. She's my _____.
2. I'm an _____. I don't have any brothers or sisters.
3. Harry and Luke share an apartment. They're _____.
4. Carolina got a divorce in 2013, but she still sees her _____.
5. It was a lovely wedding. The _____ wore a long white dress, and the _____ wore a gray suit.
6. Our next-door _____ just sold his house.
7. He's very friendly. He doesn't have an _____ in the world.
8. Her husband died, so she's a _____ to Emma, her daughter.
9. This is my _____. We're not identical, but we look alike.
10. People are really friendly here. A _____ helped me when I was lost.

◀ Go back to page 102

12C Relationship verbs

1 ▶ 12.5 Complete the sentences with the simple past form of the phrases in the box. Listen and check.

| stay in touch   go out (together)   get back together   ask (someone) out   fall in love   get along |
| have (something) in common   become friends   get married   introduce   get to know   go on a date   break up |

Couple gets back together after 30 years

Hannah Mason from the U.S. and Gustavo Ramos from Argentina first met in 1985. They were both traveling around Canada after graduating from college. A friend [1]_____ Gustavo to Hannah, and they immediately [2]_____ well. As they [3]_____ each other better, they [4]_____ good _____. They discovered that they [5]_____ a lot in _____, including a love of travel.

Friendship turned to romance when Gustavo [6]_____ Hannah _____. They [7]_____ to Gustavo's favorite restaurant in Montreal, and before long they [8]_____ in _____. They [9]_____ together for the rest of the summer, but they [10]_____ when Hannah returned to the U.S. and Gustavo went home to Argentina.

They didn't [11]_____, and that could have been the end of the story. But, 30 years later, Gustavo moved to the U.S. and contacted Hannah. They realized they still cared for each other, so it wasn't long before they [12]_____. And their story ended happily when they [13]_____ last year.

2 Choose the correct words to complete the sentences.

1. We don't *have / make / do* a lot in common; in fact, we're completely different!
2. I think I'm falling *on / in / for* love.
3. Are Charlie and Sarah really *leaving / going / getting* out together?
4. They're getting *marry / marriage / married* next year.
5. Do you get *along / in / out* well with your brother?
6. My boss introduced me *with / for / to* my future wife.
7. The first date that we went *to / in / on* together was to a rock concert.
8. They had a big argument and decided to break *up / off / out*.
9. We were classmates, but we only *became / got / came* friends after we graduated from high school.
10. I first *became / arrived / got to know* her when we worked together in Istanbul.
11. Has Sam ever asked you *out / up / off* for dinner?
12. James and I are thinking of *going / getting / joining* back together.
13. You'll have to *go / have / stay* in touch while you're away.

◀ Go back to page 106

157

COMMUNICATION PRACTICE

7A Student A

1. Student B has recently moved to an apartment in another country. Find out if he/she has done these things.

   A *Have you unpacked your things yet?*
   B *Yes I have. The apartment looks great.*

   1. unpack your things
   2. set up the Wi-Fi
   3. meet your neighbors
   4. explore the local area
   5. check out public transportation
   6. open a bank account

2. You are going to Miami, Florida on vacation tomorrow. Look at your "to do" list and answer Student B's questions.

   Things to do
   find my passport — ✓ (five minutes ago—on my desk)
   pack the suitcase — ✗
   reserve a hotel room — ✓ (Grand Beach Hotel, Miami)
   buy some sunscreen — ✓ (went to the store an hour ago)
   ask friend to take care of pet — ✗
   decide what to do in Miami — ✓ (city tour & shopping)

7C Student A

1. Complete the sentences with the present perfect form of the verbs in the box and *for* or *since*. Guess the correct options and tell Student B. He/She will tell you if you are correct.

   have   collect   be   take

   HOLLYWOOD FACTS

   1. The Academy Awards ceremony has _____ place _____ 1929. The winner of the Best Actor award that year was *an American / a German / a Russian* actor, Emil Jannings.
   2. The actor Johnny Depp _____ _____ *Barbie dolls / teddy bears / toy cars* _____ his daughter was little.
   3. Hollywood actress Christina Ricci _____ _____ afraid of *plants / spiders / flying* _____ most of her life.
   4. The actress Angelina Jolie _____ _____ *Chinese classes / a pilot's license / a pet snake* _____ more than ten years.

2. Listen to Student B's sentences and tell him/her if they are correct.

   1. There has been a big Hollywood sign in Los Angeles since 1923, but the first sign said "Hollywoodland."
   2. *Spider-Man* actor, Tobey Maguire, and Leonardo DiCaprio have known each other since they were children.
   3. Actress Mila Kunis has played video games for many years.
   4. Eva Marie Saint, who won an Oscar for *On the Waterfront* in 1954, has lived in Hollywood for over 60 years and still works as an actress.

8A Student A

1. You are going to cook a big meal for a group of friends. Student B will tell you what ingredients he/she has. Look at the list of ingredients and use the phrases in the box to help you reply.

   Great, that's enough.   That's too much.   That's too many.
   That's not enough.   We (only) need ...

2. You are going to cook a big meal for a group of friends. Tell Student B what ingredients you have. He/She will tell you if you need more, less, or if it is enough.

   I have 500 grams of shrimp.

   INGREDIENTS
   4 cans tomatoes
   1.5 kg. beef
   2 red peppers
   3 onions
   1 pineapple
   500 g. strawberries
   2 cartons vanilla ice cream
   2 l. orange juice

COMMUNICATION PRACTICE

8C Student A

1 You and Student B are starting work as cooks in a school cafeteria. Guess the missing words. Student B will tell you if you are correct.

SCHOOL KITCHEN GOLDEN RULES!

HYGIENE

1 You have to wear _____ at all times, but you don't have to wear gloves.

2 You can't wear _____ in the kitchen.

3 You have to wash your hands before starting to cook.

COOKING

4 You have to use _____ in all the dishes, and you can't use too much salt or sugar.

5 You have to wash all _____ , but you don't have to wash the meat.

6 You have to throw away _____ in the black trash cans.

MENU

7 You have to prepare one vegetarian dish every day.

8 You don't have to serve _____ on Fridays.

9 On Thursdays, you have to make a curry, but you can't make the sauce _____ .

10 On Wednesdays, you have to make a Chinese dish, but you can't make _____ .

8D Student A

1 Invite Student B to one of the events below. If he/she refuses, try another one.

Die Meistersinger von Nürnberg Fri 6:00 p.m.
Over four hours of German opera at the National Theater

Pencils through the ages Sat 11:00 a.m.
A talk about the history of pencils at the City Museum

Local chess competition Mon 1:00 p.m.
32 local players compete to win the tournament

Karaoke night Tue 7:00 p.m.
Sing your favorite songs all night

2 Student B is going to invite you to some events. Refuse as politely as possible every time.

9A Student A

1 Complete the quiz questions with *used to* and the verbs in parentheses.

Before they were famous

1 The singer, Madonna, _____ (work) in a donut shop. **True** or False?

2 The actor, Brad Pitt, _____ (dress up) as a chicken to advertise a fast-food restaurant. **True** or False?

3 The founder of Microsoft, Bill Gates, _____ (sell) hot dogs at his local baseball stadium. True or **False**? (He used to work as a computer programmer.)

4 The actor, Johnny Depp, _____ (feed) the penguins at a zoo in Kentucky. True or **False**? (He used to sell pens.)

5 The actor and comedian, Jim Carrey, _____ (live) with his family in a VW camper van. **True** or False?

6 The hip hop artist, Kanye West, _____ (work) as a salesperson in GAP. **True** or False?

7 The actor, Tom Cruise, _____ (work) as a chef in a Chinese restaurant. True or **False**? (He used to work in a hotel, carrying luggage for guests.)

8 Actress Julia Roberts and former U.S. president, Barack Obama, _____ (sell) ice cream. **True** or False?

2 Take turns reading your quiz questions to your partner. The correct answers are in **bold**.

9C Student A

1 Complete sentences 1–6 with the passive form of the verbs in parentheses.

1 Which famous article of clothing _____ by Dorothy in the movie *The Wizard of Oz*? (wear)
a A pair of blue boots   b A green hat   c **A pair of red shoes**

2 When _____ the first *Superman* comic _____? (publish)
a In 1901   b **In 1938**   c In 1959

3 In 2015, some drums that belonged to Ringo Starr from The Beatles were sold at auction. How much _____ they _____ for? (sell)
a **$1.75M**   b $5.5M   c $800,000

4 Who _____ the picture *Guernica* _____ by? (paint)
a Andy Warhol   b Salvador Dalí   c **Pablo Picasso**

5 Who _____ the movie *Star Wars: The Force Awakens* _____ by? (direct)
a Steven Spielberg   b **J.J. Abrams**   c George Lucas

6 Who _____ the songs "Umbrella" and "Diamonds" _____ by? (sing)
a Beyoncé   b **Rihanna**   c Lady Gaga

2 **A** Read your questions and the three possible answers to Student B. He/She has to answer. The correct answers are in **bold**.

B Try to answer Student B's questions.

163

COMMUNICATION PRACTICE

10A Student A

1 A Guess the past perfect verbs to complete the sentences.

Kevin's roommates were really angry with him because …
1 he _____ all the food in the refrigerator.
2 he _____ to the supermarket.
3 he _____ the dirty dinner dishes.
4 he _____ all the milk.
5 he _____ the kitchen.

B Read your sentences to Student B. He/She will tell you if you are correct.

2 Listen to Student B's sentences. Tell him/her if they are correct or not.

Last night, Miriam's friends planned a party for her. She was really surprised because …
1 nobody had told her about it.
2 she hadn't seen some of her friends for years!
3 everyone had bought her a present.
4 she thought her friends had forgotten about her birthday.
5 all her friends had shouted "surprise!" when she came in.

10C Student A

1 You're a journalist. You interviewed Student B last week and took notes. Check the information with him/her and correct any mistakes.

A *Did you say that you were originally from South Africa?*
B *No, I told you that I was originally from Kenya.*

> Student B
> is originally from ~~South Africa~~ Kenya.
> has lived in Argentina for ten years.
> is married and has two children.
> can't speak Spanish.
> is going to the U.S. next week.
> studied dance in the Netherlands.

2 Student B is a journalist who interviewed you last week. Correct what he/she says using the information.

B *Did you tell me that you were Irish?*
A *No, I said that I was Scottish.*

> You're Scottish.
> You moved to Kyoto in 2010.
> You're learning to speak Japanese.
> You've been to China twice.
> You're going to take part in a marathon.
> You won't go to the Olympics next year.

10D Student A

1 You are a passenger at an airport. Follow the diagram and use the phrases in the box to have a conversation with the information desk assistant.

> Excuse me, I was hoping you could help me …   I'd also like to ask about …   Just one more thing.   Can I double check?
> Could you give me some information about … , please?   Could I speak to someone about … ?

Passenger (Student A)	**Information desk assistant (Student B)**
Ask if there's a delay on the 2:00 p.m. flight to Madrid.	Apologize and explain that there is a 30-minute delay on this flight.
Ask which gate the flight is leaving from and how to get there.	Say that the flight leaves from gate A22. Offer to print out an airport map.
	Check to make sure the guest is satisfied.
Ask about a store that sells newspapers and magazines.	Explain that there are lots of stores, but suggest one on the third floor that has lots of foreign language newspapers.
Thank the assistant.	Respond politely.

2 You are a receptionist in a hotel. Respond to Student B in a helpful way. Make offers and suggestions and make sure he/she is satisfied.

Guest (Student B)	**Receptionist (Student B)**
Ask about the best way to get to the bus station.	Greet the guest and explain that the quickest way is to take a taxi. Offer to call a taxi for the guest.
Thank the receptionist. Say that you need to be at the station at 4:00 p.m.	Check to make sure the guest is satisfied.
Ask the receptionist about a good place to have lunch.	Recommend a restaurant on Main Street. Give the guest a map and explain how to get there.
Thank the receptionist.

164

COMMUNICATION PRACTICE

11C Student A

1 A Complete the questions with the correct article: *a*, *an*, *the,* or – (no article).

1 Is _____ stress _____ big problem for you and your friends?
2 What's _____ best way to get _____ good job?
3 Have you ever been to _____ U.S. or _____ Canada?

4 What did you have for _____ dinner _____ last night?
5 Would you like to take _____ English classes on _____ Internet?
6 When was _____ last time you went to _____ movies?

B Ask Student B the questions and listen to his/her answers.

12A Student A

1 Ask and answer questions with Student B to complete the crossword puzzle. Use the phrases in the box to make definitions with relative clauses.

B *What's 3 down?*
A *It's someone who is the leader of a country.*

> It's someone who/that ...   It's a place where ...
> It's something that ...

12C Student A

1 Answer Student B's questions. Use the chart below. Tell him/her where you went and what you did.

B *What did you do yesterday?*
A *First, I went to the bank to take out some money.*
B *What did you do after that?*

Where	Why
the bank	take out some money
the mall	buy a new coat
the doctor	get some test results
the market	get some fish
a café	meet some friends
the airport	pick up a friend from Washington

2 Ask Student B questions about what he/she did yesterday. Write down his/her answers in the chart below.

A *What did you do yesterday?*
B *First, I went for a swim at the sports center.*
A *What did you do after that?*

Where	Why
the sports center	*go for a swim*
the office	
the garage	
the hospital	
the hairdresser's	
the movie theater	

12D Student A

1 Thank, congratulate, or compliment Student B using phrases 1–5. Listen to his/her responses.

1 Wow, what a great presentation!
2 Your English is really good.
3 Thank you for dinner. It was delicious.
4 You found my wallet. Thanks a million!
5 Thanks so much for your help with the report.

2 Listen to Student B's ways of saying thanks or congratulations, or giving compliments. Respond using the phrases in the box.

> Thanks, it's just a secondhand one, though.
> It was a pleasure. They're lots of fun.
> Thanks. Yours is really nice, too!
> Oh, it's just something I did when I was in college.
> It wasn't just me. We're a team.

165

COMMUNICATION PRACTICE

7A Student B

1 You have recently moved to an apartment in another country. Look at your "to do" list and answer Student A's questions.

Things to do
meet your neighbors ✓ (they're very nice)
open a bank account ✗
explore the local area ✓ (got back 15 minutes ago)
unpack your things ✓ (the apartment looks great!)
set up the Wi-Fi ✗
check out pubic transportation ✓ (went this morning)

2 Student A is going to Buenos Aires on vacation tomorrow. Find out if he/she has done these things.

B *Have you bought some sunscreen yet?*
A *Yes. I went to the store an hour ago.*

1 buy some sunscreen
2 decide what to do in Buenos Aires
3 reserve a hotel room
4 find your passport
5 ask a friend to take care of your pet
6 pack your suitcase

7C Student B

1 Listen to Student A's sentences and tell him/her if they are correct.

1 The Academy Awards ceremony has taken place since 1929. The winner of the Best Actor award that year was a German actor, Emil Jannings.
2 The actor Johnny Depp has collected Barbie dolls since his daughter was little.
3 Hollywood actress Christina Ricci has been afraid of plants for most of her life.
4 The actress Angelina Jolie has had a pilot's license for more than ten years.

2 Complete the sentences with the present perfect form of the verbs in the box and *for* or *since*. Guess the correct options and tell Student A. He/She will tell you if you are correct.

know   play   be   live

HOLLYWOOD FACTS

1 There _____ _____ a big Hollywood sign in Los Angeles _____ *1923 / 1953 / 1973*, but the first sign said "Hollywoodland."
2 *Spider-Man* actor, Tobey Maguire, and *Leonardo DiCaprio / Kanye West / Joaquin Phoenix* _____ _____ each other _____ they were children.
3 Actress Mila Kunis _____ _____ *golf / video games / chess* _____ many years.
4 Eva Marie Saint, who won an Oscar for *On the Waterfront* in 1954, _____ _____ in Hollywood _____ over 60 years and still works as *a designer / an actress / a musician*.

8A Student B

1 You are going to cook a big meal for a group of friends. Tell Student A what ingredients you have. He/She will tell you if you need more, less, or if it is enough.

I have six cans of tomatoes.

2 You are going to cook a big meal for a group of friends. Student A will tell you what ingredients he/she has. Look at the list of ingredients and use the phrases in the box to help you reply.

Great, that's enough.   That's too much.
That's too many.   That's not enough.
We (only) need …

INGREDIENTS
1 whole salmon
500 g. shrimp
1 lettuce
1 cucumber
250 g. butter
1 l. milk
200 g. flour
1 coconut

COMMUNICATION PRACTICE

8C Student B

1 You and Student A are starting work as cooks in a school cafeteria. Guess the missing words. Student A will tell you if you are correct.

SCHOOL KITCHEN GOLDEN RULES!

HYGIENE

1 You have to wear <u>a hat</u> at all times, but you don't have to wear _____ .

2 You can't wear <u>jewelry</u> in the kitchen.

3 You have to wash _____ before starting to cook.

COOKING

4 You have to use <u>fresh ingredients</u> in all the dishes, and you can't use _____ .

5 You have to wash all <u>raw fruit and vegetables</u>, but you don't have to wash the _____ .

6 You have to throw away <u>all burned food</u> in the black trash cans.

MENU

7 You have to prepare _____ every day.

8 You don't have to serve <u>salad</u> on Fridays.

9 On Thursdays, you have to make a _____ , but you can't make the sauce <u>too spicy</u>.

10 On Wednesdays, you have to make _____ , but you can't make <u>sweet-and-sour sauce</u>.

8D Student B

1 Student A is going to invite you to some events. Refuse as politely as possible every time.

2 Invite Student A to one of these events. If he/she refuses, try another one.

Black-and-white night   **Thur 6:00 p.m.**
Enjoy three movies from the 1930s at Roxy Movie Theater

Crazy burger buffet   **Fri 7:00 p.m.**
Eat as many hamburgers as you want for $12

Ballroom dancing lessons   **Sat 11:00 a.m.**
Learn how to dance the waltz and cha-cha-cha

Benches of the world   **Sat 5:00 p.m.**
An exhibition of Michael Lamb's photographs of benches

9A Student B

1 Complete the quiz questions with *used to* and the verbs in parentheses.

Before they were famous

1 Famous singer, Beyoncé, _____ (sweep up) hair in her mom's beauty salon. **True** or False?

2 The actress, Jennifer Aniston, _____ (clean) salmon in a fish factory. True or **False**? (She used to clean toilets.)

3 The Australian actor, Hugh Jackman, _____ (teach) gym class at a school in England. **True** or False?

4 The actor, Tom Hanks, _____ (sell) popcorn and peanuts at his local movie theater. **True** or False?

5 The singer, Lady Gaga, _____ (work) in a library. True or **False**? (She used to work in a Greek restaurant.)

6 The actor, Sylvester Stallone, _____ (clean) the lions' cages at Central Park Zoo in New York. **True** or False?

7 The Rolling Stones singer, Mick Jagger, _____ (be) a firefighter in London. True or **False**? (He used to work in a hospital.)

8 The Russian billionaire, Roman Abramovich, _____ (sell) plastic ducks in a market. **True** or False?

2 Take turns reading your quiz questions to your partner. The correct answers are in **bold**.

9C Student B

1 Complete sentences 1–6 with the passive form of the verbs in parentheses.

1 What famous articles of clothing _____ by Harrison Ford in the *Indiana Jones* movies? (wear)
  a A hat and raincoat   b **A hat and leather jacket**   c A baseball jacket and cap

2 When _____ the first Sherlock Holmes story _____? (publish)
  a In 1810   b **In 1887**   c In 1935

3 In 2011, one of Marilyn Monroe's dresses was sold at auction. How much _____ it _____ for? (buy)
  a $1.3M   b $3.2M   c **$4.6M**

4 Who _____ the sunflower pictures _____ by? (paint)
  a **Vincent Van Gogh**   b Henri Matisse   c Salvador Dalí

5 What type of car _____ by the mad scientist Doc Brown in the *Back to the Future* movies? (drive)
  a A Lamborghini   b A Ferrari   c **A DeLorean**

6 Who _____ the movies *Titanic* and *Avatar* _____ by? (direct)
  a **James Cameron**   b Steven Spielberg   c Ridley Scott

2 **A** Try to answer Student A's questions.

  B Read your questions and the three possible answers to Student A. He/She has to answer. The correct answers are in **bold**.

171

COMMUNICATION PRACTICE

10A Student B

1 Listen to Student A's sentences. Tell him/her if they are correct or not.

Kevin's roommates were really angry with him because …
1 he had eaten all the food in the refrigerator.
2 he hadn't been to the supermarket.
3 he hadn't washed the dirty dinner dishes.
4 he had drunk all the milk.
5 he hadn't cleaned up the kitchen.

2 A Guess the past perfect verbs to complete the sentences.
Last night, Miriam's friends planned a party for her. She was really surprised because …
1 nobody _____ her about it.
2 she _____ some of her friends for years!
3 everyone _____ her a present.
4 she thought her friends _____ about her birthday.
5 all her friends _____ "surprise!" when she came in.

B Read your sentences to Student A. He/She will tell you if you are correct.

10C Student B

1 Student A is a journalist who interviewed you last week. Correct what he/she says using the information.

A *Did you say that you were originally from South Africa?*
B *No, I told you that I was originally from Kenya.*

> You're originally from Kenya.
> You've lived in Argentina for eight years.
> You're married and have one child.
> You can speak Spanish fluently.
> You're going to the U.S. next week.
> You studied dance in Belgium.

2 You are a journalist. You interviewed Student A last week and took notes. Check the information with him/her and correct any mistakes.

B *Did you tell me that you were Irish?*
A *No, I said that I was Scottish.*

> Student A
> is ~~Irish~~ Scottish.
> moved to Tokyo in 2010.
> is learning to speak Japanese.
> hasn't been to China before.
> is going to take part in a 10-km. race.
> will go to the Olympics next year if it's possible.

10D Student B

1 You work on an information desk in an airport. Respond to Student A in a helpful way. Make offers and suggestions and make sure he/she is satisfied.

Passenger (Student A)	Information desk assistant (Student B)
Ask if there's a delay on the 2:00 p.m. flight to Madrid. →	Apologize and explain that there's a 30-minute delay on this flight.
Ask which gate the flight is leaving from and how to get there. ←	Say that the flight leaves from gate A22. Offer to print out an airport map.
	Check to make sure the guest is satisfied.
Ask about a store that sells newspapers and magazines. →	Explain that there are lots of stores, but suggest one on the third floor that has lots of foreign language newspapers.
Thank the assistant. →	Respond politely.

2 You are a guest staying at a hotel. Follow the diagram and use the phrases in the box to have a conversation with the receptionist.

> Excuse me, I was hoping you could help me …   I'd also like to ask about …   Just one more thing.   Can I double check?
> Could you give me some information about … , please?   Could I speak to someone about … ?

Guest (Student B)	Receptionist (Student A)
Ask about the best way to get to the train station. →	Greet the guest and explain that the quickest way is to take a taxi. Offer to call a taxi for the guest.
Thank the receptionist. Say that you need to be at the station at 4:00 p.m. ←	Check to make sure the guest is satisfied.
Ask the receptionist about a good place to have lunch. →	Recommend a restaurant on Main Street. Give the guest a map and explain how to get there.
Thank the receptionist. →	Respond politely.

COMMUNICATION PRACTICE

11C Student B

1 A Complete the questions with the correct article: *a, an, the,* or – (no article).

1 Do you have _____ pet? What's _____ pet's name?
2 How many times _____ year do you see _____ dentist?
3 Do you like _____ reading? Are you reading _____ book right now?
4 What time do you usually go to _____ bed at _____ night?
5 What's _____ worst food you've ever had in _____ restaurant?
6 Do you know anyone who is _____ architect or _____ designer?

B Ask Student A the questions and listen to his/her answers.

12A Student B

1 Ask and answer questions with Student A to complete the crossword puzzle. Use the phrases in the box to make definitions with relative clauses.

A *What's 3 across?*
B *It's a place where you can play soccer or go for a walk.*

> It's someone who ...   It's a place where ...
> It's something that ...

12C Student B

1 Ask Student A questions about what he/she did yesterday. Write down his/her answers in the chart below.

B *What did you do yesterday?*
A *First, I went to the bank to take out some money.*
B *What did you do after that?*

Where	Why
the bank	to take out some money
the mall	
the doctor	
the market	
a café	
the airport	

2 Answer Student A's questions. Use the chart below. Tell him/her where you went and what you did.

A *What did you do yesterday?*
B *First, I went to the sports center to go for swim.*
A *What did you do after that?*

Where	Why
the sports center	go for a swim
the office	finish a report
the garage	fix my car
the hospital	visit my uncle
the hairdresser's	have my hair cut
the movie theater	see the new *Batman* movie

12D Student B

1 Listen to Student A's ways of saying thanks or congratulations, or giving compliments. Respond using the phrases in the box.

> No problem. I enjoyed working on it!
> It was no trouble at all. It was in my car.
> Do you think so? I didn't have much time to practice.
> Thanks, but I still need to improve.
> Well, thank you for coming to visit us!

2 Thank, congratulate, or compliment Student A using phrases 1–5. Listen to his/her responses.

1 Did you paint this picture? It's fantastic.
2 I'm very grateful for your help at this difficult time.
3 I love your watch! It's cool.
4 Thanks for taking care of the children.
5 Congratulations on your new car.

COMMUNICATION PRACTICE

11A Both students

1 In pairs, complete the sentences with the infinitive
or the *–ing* form of the verbs in parentheses.

Tell me about ...

1 something important you need _____ this week. (do)

2 a place you're planning _____ soon. (visit)

3 something you spend a lot of time _____ . (do)

4 a person you'd like _____ more often. (see)

5 something you can't afford _____ , but would love to have. (buy)

6 a household chore you can't stand _____ . (do)

7 a movie you're looking forward to _____ at the movie theater. (see)

8 a mistake you keep _____ in English. (make)

9 a food you would miss _____ if you lived in another country. (eat)

10 someone you expect _____ later today. (see)

2 In pairs, take turns asking and answering the questions.

A *Tell me about something important you need to do this week.*

B *I need to buy a birthday card for my mom. What about you?*

A *I need to take my car to the garage.*

IRREGULAR VERBS

Infinitive	Simple past	Past participle	Infinitive	Simple past	Past participle
be	was, were	been	make	made	made
become	became	become	meet	met	met
begin	began	begun	pay	paid	paid
bite	bit	bitten	put	put	put
break	broke	broken	read (/rid/)	read (/red/)	read (/red/)
bring	brought	brought	ride	rode	ridden
build	built	built	ring	rang	rung
buy	bought	bought	rise	rose	risen
choose	chose	chosen	run	ran	run
come	came	come	say	said	said
cost	cost	cost	see	saw	seen
do	did	done	sell	sold	sold
dream	dreamed/dreamt	dreamed/dreamt	send	sent	sent
forbid	forbade	forbidden	sleep	slept	slept
forget	forgot	forgotten	speak	spoke	spoken
forgive	forgave	forgiven	spend	spent	spent
get	got	gotten	stand	stood	stood
give	gave	given	steal	stole	stolen
go	went	gone	stick	stuck	stuck
grow	grew	grown	swim	swam	swum
have	had	had	take	took	taken
hear	heard	heard	teach	taught	taught
hide	hid	hidden	tell	told	told
hold	held	held	think	thought	thought
keep	kept	kept	throw	threw	thrown
know	knew	known	understand	understood	understood
learn	learned	learned	wake	woke	woken
leave	left	left	wear	wore	worn
let	let	let	win	won	won
lose	lost	lost	write	wrote	written

Personal Best

American English

Workbook

B1
Pre-intermediate

UNIT 7

City living

7A — LANGUAGE

GRAMMAR: Present perfect with *yet* and *already*

1 Order the words to make sentences. There may be more than one correct answer.

1 the / for / already / I've / tickets / paid

_____.

2 you / have / finished / essay / yet / your

_____?

3 it's / I've / 7 a.m. and / the house / cleaned / already

_____.

4 already / spoken / the phone / I've / to Carolina on

_____.

5 dinner / you / had / have / your / yet

_____?

6 gotten / home / she / from work / hasn't / yet

_____.

7 already / done it / have to / you don't / go shopping / because I've

_____.

8 you / Pedro's girlfriend / yet / met / have

_____?

2 Complete the sentences with the verbs in the box. Use the present perfect or simple past and the words in parentheses.

> eat   not open   spend   not make
> not take (x2)

1 The bread's not ready. I _____ it out of the oven. (yet)

2 I was going to have some chocolate, but you've _____ it. (already)

3 Camila _____ any friends at her new school _____. (yet)

4 This morning I gave both children $20 and they _____ it. (already)

5 I'm hot and sweaty because I _____ a shower _____. (yet)

6 They built the new sports stadium, but they _____ it _____. (yet)

VOCABULARY: City features

3 Are the following sentences true (T) or false (F)?

1 You usually find bridges under the ground. ____

2 You can make statues out of stone. ____

3 Traffic lights control the movement of cars. ____

4 Fountains send water into the air. ____

5 Apartment buildings are always low buildings. ____

6 At an intersection, one street meets another. ____

4 Complete the words. The first letters are given.

1 In towns and cities, it's safer to walk on the s___ ___ ___ ___ ___ ___.

2 You can cross the street at the c___ ___ ___ ___ ___ ___ ___ ___.

3 Is there a t___ ___ ___   c___ ___ I can put this empty bottle in?

4 The street was very dark because there were no s ___ ___ ___ ___ ___ ___ ___ ___ ___ ___ ___.

5 We drove through a long t___ ___ ___ ___ ___ under the river.

6 Let's sit on this b___ ___ ___ ___ to eat our sandwiches.

PRONUNCIATION: *just* and *yet*

5 ▶ 7.1 Listen to the sentences. Which sound do the underlined words start with? Write numbers 1–7 in the correct columns. Listen again and repeat.

/ǰ/	/y/
___ ___ ___ ___	___ ___ ___

1 Is Alfonso here <u>yet</u>?

2 Have you already been to the <u>gym</u>?

3 <u>Just</u> leave it there!

4 Vini <u>usually</u> has dinner with us on Fridays.

5 He applied for a new <u>job</u>.

6 Hi! How are <u>you</u>?

7 They look so <u>young</u>!

38

SKILLS 7B

LISTENING: Listening for facts and figures

1 Read the sentences from the audio about bike riding. What type of information is missing? Match the blanks with a–f.

1 It's cheap, it's _____ and, more than anything, it's fast. _____
2 Of course, I love to walk, too, but if I go anywhere on foot, it _____ too long. _____
3 There are only about _____ people living here. _____
4 I can ride my bike from one end of town to the other in _____. _____
5 If I drive to work at _____ in the morning, it takes me half an hour. _____
6 If I ride my bike, I can get to the office at _____. _____
7 When I arrive somewhere, I don't have to look for a _____. _____
8 All in all, I probably ride my bike for about _____ a week. _____

   a time
   b verb
   c noun
   d adjective
   e duration of time
   f number

2 ▶7.2 Listen and fill in the blanks in exercise 1.

3 ▶7.3 Look at the example. Listen to these sentences. Mark where the /t/ sound links with the next word and where it is not pronounced.

1 Matt and I have already walk(ed) ten miles!
2 Bret went to Bermuda on vacation.
3 She missed the bus so she went on the train instead.
4 I don't eat meat!
5 He picked up his bag and crossed the street.

4 Order the letters to make words to complete the sentences.

1 He drove around the parking lot twice, trying to find a KRAGNIP CASPE _____.
2 We stood on the FLAMTROP _____, waiting for the train to arrive.
3 If we RTAST TOU _____ at nine o'clock, we should arrive at noon.
4 I'm driving to Marla's house, so I could give you a FILT _____.
5 I usually ride my bike there. It takes too long to go NO TOFO _____.
6 We were stuck in a RACFFIT MAJ _____ for almost an hour.
7 My favorite form of BUPCLI PARTNORTSANOT _____ is the bus.
8 HURS HURO _____ starts just before seven every morning.
9 The train was full of MOCMETURS _____ on their way to work.
10 If we leave now, we should get there NO MEIT _____.

39

7C LANGUAGE

GRAMMAR: Present perfect with *for* and *since*

1 Complete the sentences with *for* or *since*.

1 We've known Maria _____ over ten years.
2 I've been a member of this gym _____ 2014.
3 My parents haven't heard from Ben _____ March.
4 Have you seen Jack _____ you arrived?
5 I've been waiting here _____ ages!
6 Aline has been sick _____ over three weeks now.
7 I haven't driven _____ I passed my test.
8 They've lived in the same apartment _____ years.
9 Pablo hasn't eaten meat _____ he was a child.
10 Have you two known each other _____ a long time?

2 Complete the questions and answers.

1 **A** How many years was she a teacher?
  B She _____ a teacher _____ three years.
2 **A** How long were you in the hospital?
  B I _____ there _____ two months.
3 **A** How long _____ Gabriela _____ a vegetarian?
  B For ten years.
4 **A** How many years _____ you and Peter _____ married?
  B For nearly five.
5 **A** How long _____ your father in the army?
  B From 1990 to 2005.
6 **A** How long _____ you study medicine?
  B I studied _____ eight years, until 2014.

3 Use the prompts to write questions and answers. Use the present perfect form of the verbs with *for* or *since*.

1 **A** how long / you / live / in Madrid
   _____?
   B I / be / here / three years
   _____.

2 **A** how long / she / be / asleep
   _____?
   B she / be / asleep / 5:30
   _____.

3 **A** how long / Luis / have / a cough
   _____?
   B he / have / it / the weekend
   _____.

4 **A** how long / your cousins / work / in France
   _____?
   B they / work there / over ten months
   _____.

PRONUNCIATION: *for* and *since*

4 ▶ 7.4 Practice saying the sentences. Are *for* and *since* stressed (S) or unstressed (U)? Listen, check, and repeat.

1	I've been here for three hours.	S	U
2	She's been sick since Wednesday.	S	U
3	We've known about it since noon.	S	U
4	Livia has lived in Paris for six months.	S	U
5	They haven't heard from her since April.	S	U
6	I haven't eaten since breakfast.	S	U
7	We haven't seen Maria for years.	S	U
8	She's been away since 2014.	S	U

SKILLS 7D

WRITING: Writing an essay

1 Read Otto's essay and complete it with these linking words and phrases.

a The second reason   c First
b In conclusion   d Finally

Should cars be banned from the downtown area?

I live in a beautiful, historic city, but everyone agrees that there is a problem with traffic. Every day, over 60,000 people drive downtown to work or study, and pollution levels are rising. Our local council has suggested banning all cars from the downtown area. Personally, I think this is a very bad idea.

1 ____, how would people get to work? Houses in the city are very expensive, and people who live in the suburbs or outside the city already have long trips to work. In my opinion, it is unreasonable that they should have to wait for a bus to get downtown.

2 ____ is that I don't believe it's possible for everyone to use public transportation, walk, or ride their bikes to work. For example, people in wheelchairs need special vehicles, and many people have to carry heavy tools or equipment for their work.

3 ____, I'm worried that local stores and businesses will suffer. If people can't drive to the stores, they won't go at all. Most people don't want to carry bags full of shopping on a bus.

4 ____, I feel that banning cars from downtown is a bad idea. I would say that we should be looking at different ways of reducing pollution—ways that don't involve making life difficult for people! For example, we should develop better electric cars, improve public transportation, and make better bike lanes.

2 Find these phrases in Otto's essay. Then write sentences with your own ideas about whether or not cars should be banned from the downtown area.

1 Personally, _____.
2 In my opinion _____.
3 I don't believe that _____.
4 I'm worried that _____.
5 I would say that _____.

3 Use the words in the box to complete the arguments against Otto's opinion.

fresh air   pollution   healthier   safe
public transportation   permission

1 In my opinion, banning cars would reduce _____.

2 I don't believe that it's _____ for cars and bicycles to share the streets.

3 I think that getting some _____ by walking or riding a bike to work is a good idea.

4 People who need to carry heavy equipment could get _____ from the council to drive.

5 Personally, I feel that people who can't walk or ride a bike should use _____.

6 I wouldn't say that riding a bike is difficult for most people, and it makes them _____.

4 Write an essay giving the opposite opinion to Otto's.

- Use ideas from exercise 3 or your own ideas.
- Organize your ideas into five paragraphs: introduction, reasons 1–3, conclusion.
- Give examples or evidence to support your opinion.
- Use some of the phrases from exercises 2 and 3.

7 REVIEW and PRACTICE

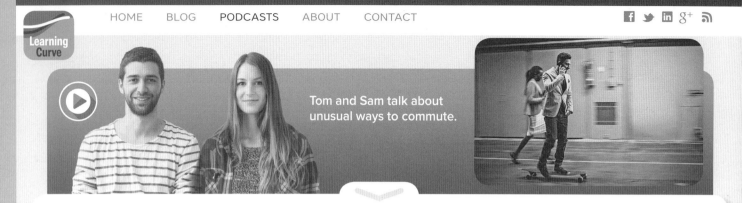

LISTENING

1 ▶ 7.5 Listen to the podcast. What does the speaker say is the main advantage of how he commutes?

　a　It's a healthy way to get to work.
　b　His trip is quicker than other people's.
　c　He can still wear a suit when he's traveling.

2 ▶ 7.5 Listen again. Complete the sentences with one or two words.

1　It takes Louie about _____ to get to work.
2　He rides his skateboard on the _____.
3　He has been skateboarding for _____ years.
4　He thinks other people are _____ of his trip to work.
5　He says the best thing about not using _____ is not waiting for buses.
6　He thinks skateboarding is less _____ than riding a bike.
7　He also uses his skateboard to go to _____.

READING

1 Read the blog about car-free cities. Match 1–4 with paragraphs A–D.

1　places where little is being done to reduce the use of cars　____
2　how some cities have encouraged people not to drive　____
3　how technology can help people manage without cars　____
4　a new city where people won't need to drive　____

2 Are the sentences true (T), false (F), or is there not enough information to decide (N)?

1　People often need to drive to other places on their way to and from work.　____
2　Most people who work in cities drive to work.　____
3　In Milan, most people travel by public transportation once or twice a week.　____
4　London is a safe place to ride a bike to work.　____
5　In the new town near Chengdu, it will be easy for most people to walk everywhere.　____
6　Planners want people who work in Chengdu to drive there very quickly in their own cars.　____
7　It is easy for people in Helsinki to get information to help them travel without cars.　____
8　Most people in Helsinki already use public transportation.　____
9　Currently people in some U.S. cities prefer to ride their bikes around town.　____
10　In Sydney, town planning makes it easy for people to use cars rather than public transportation.　____

REVIEW and PRACTICE 7

HOME BLOG PODCASTS ABOUT CONTACT

Guest blogger Penny writes about how cities are designed.

Car-free cities: dream or reality?

What's the number one thing you hate about cities? It's probably the traffic. Who wants to breathe in dirty air all day, or spend hours stuck in a traffic jam on their daily commute? On the other hand, we've had cars for over 100 years now and we rely on them, especially with our busy lives—rushing to drop the kids off at school before we go to work, or going to the supermarket on the way home. So how can town planners persuade us to leave our cars at home? Here are some different ideas from around the world.

A Since 2014, Milan has had a really interesting system: for every day that residents leave their car at home, they get a voucher for the value of a ticket on the train or bus! And in Copenhagen, around half of all workers commute by bike on a huge, safe network of bike lanes. Perhaps London should try to do the same. Traffic there moves more slowly than the average bike rider, but the streets are far more dangerous on two wheels!

B In some countries, town planners working on new towns and cities are trying to reduce the use of cars to a bare minimum before they've even been built. For example, one new town in China, with a planned population of 80,000, is being designed so that all its stores, entertainment venues, work places, etc. are within a fifteen-minute walk from where residents live. And there'll be fast public transportation connections to the nearest big city of Chengdu.

C In Helsinki, local authorities are using phone apps to reduce car numbers. The city has several schemes for people to share the use of bikes and cars. The app allows anyone to quickly find the nearest shared bike, car, or taxi, or tells them the best and fastest bus or train route. Planners there hope that within ten years no one will need to drive in the city at all.

D Sadly, not all cities are encouraging car-free trips. It's true that 60% of people living in Paris don't own a car, but many U.S. towns and cities are designed specifically for the use of cars. And there aren't any alternatives yet. And in car-loving Sydney, things seem to be going backward. There are plans to get rid of pedestrian space to make room for even more cars!

UNIT 8 Food for thought

8A — LANGUAGE

GRAMMAR: *Too, too many, too much,* and *(not) enough*

1 Match the pairs of sentences.

1	She needs a vacation. ____	a	She works too hard.
2	I can't wear this sweater on a warm day. ____	b	It's too hot in here.
3	She felt uncomfortable after the meal. ____	c	It's not thick enough.
4	Can you open the window? ____	d	She doesn't work hard enough.
5	Let's turn the central heating on. ____	e	She didn't eat enough.
6	This coat's no good for winter. ____	f	It isn't warm enough in here.
7	She won't pass the exam. ____	g	It's too thick.
8	She was hungry when she went to bed. ____	h	She ate too much.

2 Complete the conversation with *too, too many, too much,* or *(not) enough*.

A I'm so worried about my final grades. I haven't done ¹_____ work.

B I feel the same! I think I'm taking ²_____ classes. I work late every evening, but then I'm ³_____ tired to concentrate in class.

A I'm especially worried about French. Our teacher doesn't explain things clearly ⁴_____, and he doesn't give us ⁵_____ time to write things down.

B My problem is history. There's ⁶_____ information to write and there's ⁷_____ time. I want to study history in college, and if my exam results aren't good ⁸_____, I won't be able to.

A Well, try not to worry about it ⁹_____!

B You're right. Getting ¹⁰_____ stressed won't help!

VOCABULARY: Food and drink

3 Order the letters to complete the words.

1	s __ __ __ __ __	MONAL
2	e __ __ __ __ __ __ __	LPGAGNT
3	p __ __ __ __	CHAE
4	a __ __ __ __ p __ __	EPPL EI
5	p __ __ __ __ __ __	PPSREE
6	f __ __ __ __ __ j __ __ __ __ __	TIUR CIUE
7	p __ __ __ __ __ __ __	EAINLEPP
8	t __ __ __ __ __ s __ __ __ __ __	MOOTA UACE
9	c __ __ __ __ __ __ __	UUMCREB
10	s __ __ __ __ __	PRMIH

4 Complete the crossword puzzle. The first letters and total number of letters are given.

Across

4 meat from a sheep (4)

5 lots of people eat this for breakfast with milk (6)

8 a soft red fruit—you can make jam with it (10)

9 a fruit with a hard brown outside and a white part and liquid inside (7)

10 meat from a cow (4)

Down

1 a round fruit that is yellow and pink (5)

2 a vegetable with lots of green leaves; we usually cook it (7)

3 meat from a large bird (6)

6 a green salad vegetable (7)

7 we use this powder to make bread, cakes, etc. (5)

PRONUNCIATION: *too much sugar*

5 ▶ 8.1 Look at the underlined words. Listen and circle the vowel sound that you hear. Listen, check, and repeat.

1	What <u>should</u> I do now?	/u/	/ə/	/ʊ/
2	There aren't <u>enough</u> strawberries.	/u/	/ə/	/ʊ/
3	I'm going to <u>cook</u> dinner.	/u/	/ə/	/ʊ/
4	May I <u>use</u> your pen?	/u/	/ə/	/ʊ/
5	Would you like a <u>cup</u> of coffee?	/u/	/ə/	/ʊ/
6	I hate tomato <u>soup</u>!	/u/	/ə/	/ʊ/
7	There wasn't any <u>food</u> left.	/u/	/ə/	/ʊ/
8	You should <u>put</u> a jacket on.	/u/	/ə/	/ʊ/

44

SKILLS 8B

READING: Scanning for specific information

Aquafaba ("Aqua what?!")

As regular readers of this blog will know, I know my food! I always say, give me a dish from pretty much anywhere in the world and, within two minutes, I'll tell you what's in it. However, this weekend, I discovered that maybe I don't know quite as much as I thought I did. A vegan friend of mine invited me over for dinner. (He turned vegan five years ago after seeing a really shocking movie on the dairy industry.) Just to remind you, vegans avoid all animal products, including honey. So I was expecting beans to be on the menu (and they were—lots of them—for the main course). But it was the dessert that took me by surprise—vegan ice cream. And how do you make ice cream, I hear you ask, without milk, cream or eggs? (I should say, how do you make nice, creamy ice cream without dairy products, because I've had some fairly unpleasant vegan ice creams in my time!) Well, it turns out that the key to good vegan ice cream, and a whole load of other desserts, is bean water. Yes, you read that correctly, bean water, i.e., the water that beans have been boiled in. (You know, the stuff you usually throw down the drain.) Bean water, my friend tells me, is called "aquafaba" by the vegan community. It's increasingly used to replace egg whites in savory and sweet vegan dishes, such as vegan butter, cheese, cookies, and cakes. And I can honestly say it works, although it does give the ice cream a slightly odd smell. It's so good, in fact, that the morning after my dinner date, I went straight to the supermarket for a can of beans. As I write, my first batch of aquafaba ice cream is firming up nicely in the freezer!

1 Underline the key words in these questions. Then scan the text about an unusual food and choose the best answer.

1 What did the blogger's friend invite her over for?
   a dessert
   b dinner
   c a dish containing eggs
2 What do vegans avoid eating?
   a milk and eggs
   b honey and cream
   c all animal products
3 What was the blogger expecting to be given to eat?
   a beans
   b vegan ice cream
   c a dessert
4 What, according to the blogger, is the key to many good vegan desserts?
   a beans
   b bean water
   c cream
5 In vegan cooking, aquafaba is used to replace
   a cream.
   b egg whites.
   c dairy products.

2 Look at the sentences. Are they true (T), false (F), or isn't there enough information to decide (N)?

1 The blogger is a vegetarian, not a vegan. _____
2 The blogger's vegan friend has never eaten animal products. _____
3 The main course of the meal included beans. _____
4 This was the first time the blogger had eaten vegan ice cream. _____
5 The blogger says that aquafaba is usually thrown away. _____
6 Aquafaba is much healthier than egg white. _____
7 She says the smell of this vegan ice cream is especially nice. _____
8 She has now tried making vegan ice cream with aquafaba herself. _____

3 Choose the correct linkers to complete the sentences. There may be more than one correct answer.

1 I liked the vegan ice cream, *however / but / although* I found the idea of bean water a little strange at first.
2 *Although / However / But* I'd tried lots of vegan ice creams, I'd never especially enjoyed them.
3 I don't have a recipe for the ice cream, *however / although / but* I'm going to follow my friend's instructions.
4 I usually know what's in a dish. *But / Although / However*, I have no idea what's in this.
5 I don't usually cook vegan food. *However / Although / But*, I feel inspired to try now.

45

8C LANGUAGE

GRAMMAR: *Have to*, *not have to*, and *can't*

1 Choose the correct options to complete the sentences.

1 You ___ finish that pie if you don't want it.
  a don't have to   b have to   c can't

2 To pass this exam, you ___ get over 75% right.
  a can't   b don't have to   c have to

3 You ___ talk to Peter because he has a lot of work to do.
  a have to   b don't have to   c can't

4 This is Ben's medicine. He ___ take it three times a day.
  a can't   b have to   c has to

5 Do we ___ bring our own food?
  a can't   b don't have to   c have to

6 I have an important meeting. I ___ be late.
  a don't have to   b can't   c have to

7 My new job is close to my house, so I ___ take the subway.
  a can't   b don't have to   c have to

8 If you hear the fire alarm, you ___ leave the building immediately.
  a don't have to   b can't   c have to

9 Why are you going home? Do you ___ get up early tomorrow?
  a have to   b don't have to   c can't

10 It's Gina's birthday next week. I ___ forget to send her a card.
  a don't have to   b can't   c have to

2 Complete the sentences with *can't*, or the correct form of (*not*) *have to*. There may be more than one correct answer.

1 We're going for a walk, but you _____ come if you're too tired.

2 There are thieves in the area, so you _____ make sure your car is locked.

3 Does Harry _____ wear his uniform on the school trip?

4 We _____ swim here; it's too dangerous.

5 Marta is very rich, so she _____ work.

6 Larry is in a hurry because he _____ leave in five minutes.

7 Do the children's parents _____ sign these forms?

8 We can leave the classroom at any time. We _____ ask for permission.

VOCABULARY: Adjectives to describe food

3 Complete the sentences with the adjectives in the box.

| creamy | salty | sour | healthy | sweet |
| crunchy | bitter | delicious | | |

1 A _____ diet should include plenty of fresh vegetables and fruit.

2 Alex is such a good cook. He made an absolutely _____ curry last week.

3 You shouldn't eat too many _____ foods like potato chips and olives.

4 Someone left the cookies out all night and they're not _____ any more.

5 The coffee was much too strong and had a pretty _____ taste.

6 Maria loves _____ foods like chocolate and cakes.

7 She served the apple pie with a lovely, _____ sauce.

8 Add sugar to the lemon juice, otherwise it will taste too _____.

4 Complete the adjectives. Some of the letters are given.

1 Laura put a lot of chilli peppers in the soup and it was too s___ ___ ___ ___.

2 Rob forgot to take the potatoes out of the oven and they were b___ ___ ___ ___ ___.

3 You haven't cooked this chicken long enough; it's still r___ ___ in the middle!

4 Paul loves un___ ___ ___ ___ ___ ___y foods like pizza and burgers.

5 You can make a t___ ___ ___y soup with chicken bones.

6 Does the restaurant use f___ ___ ___ ___ vegetables from their own garden?

7 Bean ice cream? It sounds d___ ___ ___ ___ ___ ___ing!

8 I don't eat meat. Are there any v___ ___ ___ ___ ___ ___ian dishes?

PRONUNCIATION: Sentence stress

5 ▶ 8.2 Practice saying the sentences, putting the main stress on the underlined modal verb. Listen, check, and repeat.

1 You <u>have</u> to bring your passport with you.
2 Do we <u>have</u> to leave tomorrow morning?
3 She <u>can't</u> take the hotel towels to the beach.
4 You don't <u>have</u> to wait if you don't want to.
5 Parents <u>can't</u> help their children with this homework.
6 She <u>has</u> to arrive there before 9 a.m.

SKILLS 8D

SPEAKING: Making and responding to invitations

1 ▶ 8.3 Listen to the conversation between Karen and Brigit. Complete the phrases.

1 Do _____ trying out that new Japanese restaurant tonight?
2 I'm _____ I already have _____.
3 But would you be _____ the Japanese place another evening?
4 OK then, do you _____ go on Saturday instead?
5 Oh _____, I think _____ that evening.
6 Yeah. That would be _____, except I'll have to leave early.
7 Would _____ to stay over at my place?
8 That's _____ of you, thanks.

2 Are phrases 1–8 in exercise 1 used for inviting (I), accepting (A) or refusing (R)?

1 ___
2 ___
3 ___
4 ___
5 ___
6 ___
7 ___
8 ___

3 ▶ 8.4 Listen to four people refusing invitations. Check (✓) the things each speaker does.

	Speaker 1	Speaker 2	Speaker 3	Speaker 4
Uses a pleasant intonation				
Apologizes before saying something negative				
Gives explanations				

4 ▶ 8.5 Read the conversation then complete what B says. There is more than one possible answer for each blank. Then listen and say B's part aloud during the pauses.

A Would you be interested in going to the movies on Saturday? There's a new action movie that's supposed to be really good.
B ¹_____. My parents are having a party. It's been planned for a long time, and I can't miss it.
A Oh sure, I understand. The movie's playing all week though. Do you feel like going another night?
B ²_____. I read an online review and it sounds really exciting. Sunday's good for me.
A Great. Would you like to come over to my place for a quick dinner before we go?
B ³_____. Why don't I bring something for dessert?
A Excellent! See you then. Bye for now.

47

8 REVIEW and PRACTICE

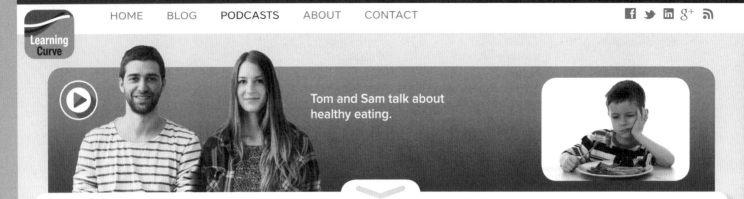

HOME   BLOG   **PODCASTS**   ABOUT   CONTACT

Tom and Sam talk about healthy eating.

LISTENING

1 ▶ 8.6 Listen to the podcast. Choose the best summary.

  a Luca's diet is healthy now, but it wasn't when he was younger.
  b Luca and his brother have unhealthy diets now.
  c Luca's diet has always been very unhealthy.

2 ▶ 8.6 Listen again. Are the sentences true (T) or false (F)?

  1 Luca's mother still tells him to eat more fish. _____
  2 When he was younger, Luca ate a lot of vegetables. _____
  3 Luca didn't use to like green vegetables. _____
  4 Luca's mother made him eat everything on his plate. _____
  5 Luca's brother doesn't like vegetables. _____
  6 Luca eats uncooked vegetables. _____
  7 Luca avoids food with a lot of salt. _____
  8 Luca eats unhealthy food while watching movies. _____
  9 Luca really dislikes fish. _____
  10 Luca's favorite sauces contain a lot of cream. _____

READING

1 Read the blog about cooking. What does it suggest?

  a Everyone can learn to cook well with the right instructions.
  b There are lots of things that can go wrong when cooking.
  c You need lots of equipment in order to cook successfully.

2 Choose the correct options, according to the information in the blog.

  1 What is the advantage of cooking a vegetable soup?
     a It is healthy.
     b It is easy.
     c It is vegetarian.
  2 Before you start cooking, what should you read?
     a the first line of the recipe
     b the first half of the recipe
     c the whole recipe
  3 Which of these things should you check before starting to cook?
     a that you have the right equipment
     b what time it is
     c how many vegetables you need
  4 What will a recipe not tell you?
     a which vegetables to use
     b what kind of knife you need
     c exactly how to prepare an onion
  5 What does the word concentrate in line 20 mean?
     a to do something quickly
     b to focus on one activity
     c to be very careful
  6 Why should you add stock to the soup?
     a to make it smell nice
     b to make it less hot
     c to improve the taste
  7 What does the last line of the blog suggest?
     a You probably won't eat the soup.
     b You will really enjoy the soup.
     c You will definitely make the soup again.

REVIEW and PRACTICE 8

HOME   BLOG   PODCASTS   ABOUT   CONTACT

Guest blogger Jack tells us how to stay calm in the kitchen.

Keep calm and go on cooking!

If you're new to cooking and want some basic tips, here's a great recipe for a simple, but delicious soup. I'll take you step by step through what to do and what not to do!

1   The first piece of advice is, <u>always</u> read the instructions to the end before you start cooking. You don't want to find out halfway through that you don't have all
5   the ingredients (What if you've run out of noodles?), or some of the equipment (What if your neighbor doesn't own an ice cream maker either?), or enough time to cook it (Oh no, my girlfriend/boyfriend
10 will be here in five minutes and all I have is a lot of raw vegetables!)

So, after you've read all the instructions, re-read the first line: "Peel and slice the onion." Take a sharp kitchen knife, and remove the first brown layer from the onion, and then the second (brownish) layer and then a third. Now, of course the recipe won't tell you when to stop and you
15 don't want to end up with a really tiny onion. Make sure you have plenty of other vegetables: a red pepper, a couple of carrots, and a potato (even if slightly green). Chop them into small pieces (and don't worry about the green potato, no one will know once it's cooked).

Next, heat some oil in a pan. But how much oil? And what kind of pan? Pour in just enough to cover the bottom of a medium-sized saucepan. Then add the vegetables. At this point, whatever
20 you do, concentrate! Do not attempt to do anything else! Do not answer your phone! Ignore the doorbell (unless it's the firefighters!) It's so easy to forget to keep an eye on things. Turn the heat down and let the vegetables cook gently for a few minutes. (Don't they smell good?) Then add a liter of water, plus two big spoons of stock (you know, that mysterious salty brown powder at the back of the cupboard. It may not look much, but without it, your soup won't taste … anything like
25 soup). Put a lid on the pan, and leave it for half an hour.

Of course, at this point, you'll forget the instruction not to answer your phone, and will end up talking to a friend for an hour. The final step (nearly) is to taste the "soup." And when you discover that even your dog won't eat it … order takeout.
29 And that's why you should always read the instructions first!

UNIT 9 Money and shopping

9A LANGUAGE

GRAMMAR: used to

1 Complete the sentences with the words and phrases in the box. You will need to use two of them twice.

> usually   use to   went   did   used to   go

1 David looks different now. He didn't _____ have long hair.
2 On my sixth birthday, I _____ horseback riding for the first time.
3 _____ you use to visit your cousins when you were younger?
4 I used to _____ to the park on Saturdays.
5 Yuri _____ takes the bus to college.
6 She ate lots of ice cream as a child. She _____ love it!
7 Did Daniel _____ be so thin?
8 Lara doesn't _____ go skiing in the summer.

2 Complete the sentences with the correct form of *used to* and the verb in parentheses.

1 I never ate olives as a child. I _____ them. (hate)
2 Did Steve _____ so hard-working when he was younger? (be)
3 She _____ tennis in her teens, but doesn't now. (play)
4 My grandfather _____ a cell phone. (not have)
5 Did your parents _____ you bedtime stories? (read)
6 I _____ bright colors in the past. (not wear)
7 Did you _____ the train to New York? (take)
8 Alice _____ so much before she went to college. (not go out)

VOCABULARY: Money verbs

3 Order the letters to make money verbs.

1 We aren't rich. We can't **fardof** _____ to stay in that hotel.
2 This café's so expensive. They **ceragh** _____ $10 for a cup of coffee!
3 She has a good job and **searn** _____ more than her husband.
4 Don't forget to **apy kabc** _____ the money Daniel gave you.
5 Jack's going shopping because he **tog apid** _____ yesterday.
6 Don't **awest** _____ your salary on things that you don't need!

4 Complete the sentences with money verbs in the correct form.

1 Can I _____ some money to buy a ticket to the concert, please?
2 How much did you _____ on that new jacket?
3 I _____ my best friend $10 yesterday to buy lunch.
4 Their house is huge. It must be _____ a fortune.
5 Which _____ more, the blue shirt or the green one?
6 I'm trying to _____ a little money each month to buy a new car.

PRONUNCIATION: used to/use to

5 ▶9.1 Practice saying the sentences. Pay attention to *used to* and *use to*. Listen, check, and repeat.

1 She didn't use to play tennis.
2 They used to love going to festivals.
3 Did you use to walk to school together?
4 We used to work out at the same gym.
5 He didn't use to like classical music.
6 I remember that you used to enjoy dancing.

50

SKILLS 9B

LISTENING: Identifying attitude and opinion

1 ▶9.2 Listen to Tom and Natalie talking about shopping. Are these sentences true (T) or false (F)?

1 Tom likes to shop online. _____
2 Natalie prefers online shopping. _____
3 Tom thinks online shopping is easy. _____
4 Natalie doesn't like department stores. _____

2 Are the underlined phrases from the conversation opinion (A), feeling (B), or attitude (C)?

1 Yeah, I do most of my shopping online. I much prefer it.
2 Sure, you see it's so convenient to shop online. _____
3 I mean, to be honest, shopping for clothes online is the opposite of convenient. _____
4 I wouldn't say that's a big problem. _____
5 I get really fed up waiting! _____
6 I guess I just like stores, especially department stores. _____
7 I enjoy wandering from the clothes section to kitchen appliances. _____
8 I just remember the crowds and the lines: it was really boring! _____

3 ▶9.2 Listen again and number the fillers 1–8 in the order you hear them.

a like _____
b I mean _____
c kind of _____
d Uh _____
e Well _____
f you see _____
g sort of _____
h So _____

4 ▶9.2 Listen again and complete these sentences and phrases with fillers from exercise 3.

1 Sure, _____, it's so convenient.
2 _____, you just return it, don't you?
3 It's _____ convenient because you don't have to leave your home.
4 You can _____ get everything you want under one roof.
5 And, _____, you can pick things up and see them and feel them.

5 Complete the sentences with shopping words.

1 That jacket was only thirty dollars? Wow! That's an absolute b___ ___ ___ ___ ___ ___!
2 I bought this bag on s___ ___ ___ for half the usual price!
3 Students get a 20% d___ ___ ___ ___ ___ ___ ___ in all our stores.
4 The pants didn't fit, so I sent them back and got a r___ ___ ___ ___ ___ ___.
5 I asked the salesperson if I could e___ ___ ___ ___ ___ ___ ___ the jacket for a larger size.
6 Are you paying with cash or by c___ ___ ___ ___ ___ card?
7 I need to try this suit on. Where's the nearest d___ ___ ___ ___ ___ ___ ___ room?
8 Sometimes I used to go w___ ___ ___ ___ ___ shopping with no money in my pocket. I just looked at all the beautiful things.
9 There was such a long l___ ___ ___ to pay that I decided not to wait.
10 I paid for the items and the cashier gave me a r___ ___ ___ ___ ___ ___.

9C LANGUAGE

GRAMMAR: The passive

1 Choose the correct options to complete the sentences.

1. The wallet was ____ yesterday by a member of the public.
   a turn in   b turned in   c to turn in
2. This park ____ by many people.
   a isn't used   b isn't using   c doesn't use
3. When was the problem ____?
   a discovering   b discovered   c discover
4. In the summer, dinner ____ on the terrace.
   a served   b is served   c serving
5. A number of mistakes ____ during the investigation.
   a was made   b made   c were made
6. Over 300 people ____ to the party.
   a were invited   b invited   c was invited

2 Complete the text about the history of money. Use the present or past passive form of the verbs in parentheses.

It ¹_____ (say) by many people today that "money makes the world go around." It's certainly hard to imagine life without it, but money ²_____ (not invent) until several thousand years ago in China. Tiny models of weapons and tools ³_____ (use) there as money. Before that, full-size tools and weapons ⁴_____ (exchange) for goods and services in a system called "barter." The first coins ⁵_____ (produce) 2,500 years ago in Lydia, in what is now Turkey. They ⁶_____ (make) from "electrum," a mixture of gold and silver. The first paper bills ⁷_____ (print) by the Chinese at around the same time. Fast forward in time, and today most goods and services ⁸_____ (buy) with credit and debit cards, or even using smartphone "wallets." Huge sums ⁹_____ (send) from bank to bank without anyone touching a single paper bill. Virtual currencies like Bitcoin ¹⁰_____ (accept) in some stores and online. Will bills and coins disappear completely during our lifetime?

3 Complete the sentences with the passive form of the verbs in the box. Use the tense in parentheses.

discover   eat   write   invent
wash   bake   steal   paint

1. The planet Uranus _____ by Sir William Herschel in 1781. (simple past)
2. Bread _____ every morning in our own bakery. (simple present)
3. I don't have a bike now. It _____ last week from outside the school. (simple past)
4. The picture _____ by Pablo Picasso in 1933. (simple past)
5. His car always looks perfect because it _____ every week. (simple present)
6. This song _____ by John Grant. (simple past)
7. Lunch _____ in the main dining room. (simple present)
8. The first electric train _____ by a German in 1879. (simple past)

PRONUNCIATION: Sentence stress

4 ▶9.3 Underline the three words that you think will be stressed in each sentence. Listen, check, and repeat.

1. This soup is made with peppers.
2. The children are taught by their parents.
3. These plants are grown by my father.
4. The message was posted on Facebook.
5. Those houses were built in 1975.
6. That race was won by her cousin.

SKILLS 9D

WRITING: Writing a formal e-mail

1 Read Elisabeth's e-mail complaining about a flat-screen TV she bought. Choose the correct words and phrases.

To: info@tvs2go.com

RE: Recent order (H23 100-A)

---

¹*Dear Sir/Madam: / Hello,*

I am writing ²*to tell you about / with regard to* the flat-screen TV that ³*a man installed / was installed* in my house last Thursday.

First, ⁴*someone delivered the TV / the TV was delivered* at 3 p.m., not at 10 a.m., as agreed. Second, as the man left, I noticed that some wires were hanging down at the back of the TV. When I ⁵*pointed this out / told him about it*, he was extremely rude. Although he agreed to fix the wires, he ⁶*did not / didn't* check to make sure the TV was working correctly.

⁷*I'm / I am* sure you will agree that this level of service is ⁸*terrible / unacceptable*, and that a full refund of the delivery charge would be appropriate. Could you please arrange ⁹*to pay the money / for the money to be paid* within a week?

I look forward to hearing from you soon.

¹⁰*Regards, / Bye for now,*

Elisabeth Miller

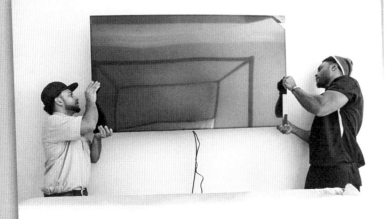

2 Match the correct options 1–10 from exercise 1 with these features of formal e-mails.

a full forms, not contractions   ___ ___
b formal words and expressions   ___ ___ ___
c passives to avoid being personal ___ ___ ___
d a formal greeting   ___
e a formal ending   ___

3 Complete the sentences with nouns made from these verbs.

| refund   argue   increase deliver |
| improve discover discuss |
| decide   organize inform |

1 Last week I made the _____ to purchase several items from your website.
2 The _____ on your website was not correct.
3 I was not aware of the price _____ when I ordered the product.
4 I was shocked by the _____ that several parts were broken.
5 After a _____ with one of your staff, I am still not satisfied.
6 I did not expect to become involved in an _____ with one of your sales team.
7 Poor service will damage the reputation of your _____.
8 Your company needs to make a big _____ in the quality of its goods.
9 I will expect _____ of a replacement within a week.
10 Please send me a _____ for the full amount of my order.

4 Write a formal e-mail complaining about a product you have bought recently.

- Include paragraphs giving the reason for writing, explaining the situation and saying what action you want taken.
- Remember to use the features in exercise 2.
- Use the sentences in exercise 3 for ideas.

53

9 REVIEW and PRACTICE

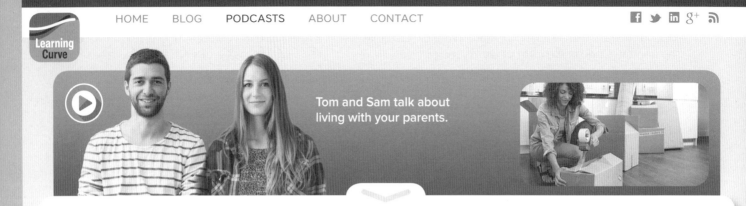

HOME   BLOG   **PODCASTS**   ABOUT   CONTACT

Tom and Sam talk about living with your parents.

LISTENING

1 ▶ 9.4 Listen to the podcast. Check (✓) the correct statement.

a Sonia moved out of her parents' house because there were too many rules. _____
b Sonia's parents gave her money to help with her college tuition. _____
c Sonia went to live with her parents because she wasn't earning enough money. _____
d Sonia couldn't afford to go to college so she got a job instead. _____

2 ▶ 9.4 Listen again. Complete the sentences with one or two words.

1 One of the _____ in Sonia's life was when she graduated from college.
2 Sonia was scared that she might trip and _____.
3 Sonia didn't know how she was going to _____ her student loan.
4 Sonia owed a total of _____ dollars.
5 It took Sonia _____ to get a good job.
6 Sonia gave her parents money for _____ and _____.
7 When she was _____, Sonia didn't like her parents' rules.

READING

1 Read the blog about money and relationships. Choose the best summary.

a Couples often break up because they can't agree about money. You should talk about money with your partner and, if you have very different attitudes, it's best not to get married.
b It's hard to change people's attitudes toward money, but if you understand how your partner feels, you won't feel so angry if he or she wastes money you wanted to save.
c Attitudes toward money are very important. You should try to understand how your partner feels and, if you have different attitudes, you should try to find ways to stop them from causing arguments.

2 Check (✓) the correct sentences, according to the information in the blog.

1 Things that happen in our lives can affect how we feel about money. _____
2 Attitudes toward money are more important than someone's personality. _____
3 People from poor families may not feel happy about borrowing money. _____
4 Attitudes toward money can change if a relationship lasts a long time. _____
5 Couples should be honest with each other when they talk about money. _____
6 We should discuss the emotional reasons why money is important to us. _____
7 People with very different attitudes toward money can't have a successful relationship. _____
8 Each person in a couple should pay the same amount of the bills. _____
9 Philip and Christa wanted to buy a home together. _____
10 When Philip saw Christa spending a lot of money, he thought their relationship wouldn't work. _____

HOME   BLOG   PODCASTS   ABOUT   CONTACT

Tom writes about money and relationships.

Money: how to stop it from ruining your relationship

Experts say that the main reason long-term couples break up is money—and the arguments it causes. Our attitudes toward money often come from our life experiences, and that makes them difficult to change. Someone brought up in a poor family may become very anxious about owing money, and be horrified at the idea of "wasting" it on things they don't think are necessary. So what can we do to stop money from ruining a relationship?

"We all have a money personality," says life coach Jo Handslip. "If we're thinking of a long-term relationship with someone, we need to get to know that side of them just as well as the other parts of their character. And whatever we may hope, we also need to understand that their money personality isn't likely to change."

The most important thing a couple can do is talk about money openly. "This isn't about money simply as a means of buying things," says Jo. "It's about what money represents to us." She says that couples should start by trying to identify what each of them associates with money, like success, security, independence, power, fun, or being free from stress.

Once they understand this, they can try to make their different attitudes work together. So, if one of you loves the freedom and excitement of spending money, and the other one wants the security of having savings, maybe you should agree to share the cost of bills, but keep the rest of your money separate. That way, the "spender" can only spend their own money, and the "saver" can feel secure. Or you could agree a maximum amount you can spend without asking your partner.

Philip Walker knows all about the problems money can cause. He and his girlfriend Christa broke up just two weeks before their wedding! "We were saving up for an apartment, so we agreed that the ceremony should be fairly small. But then I found out that instead of spending our savings on the wedding, Christa was going out to expensive nightclubs, celebrating with her friends, and buying lots of new clothes when she already had more than she needed. She'd buy the same dress or pairs of shoes in three different colors because she couldn't decide which she liked best! We ended up having a huge argument. In the end, seeing her throw our money away made me feel that she didn't see a future for us together."

UNIT 10 Sports and fitness

10A LANGUAGE

GRAMMAR: Past perfect

1 Choose the correct tenses to complete the sentences.

1 That evening, I was tired because I ____ ten kilometers in the afternoon.
   a had run   b ran   c was running

2 We ____ hungry because we'd already eaten.
   a weren't being   b hadn't been   c weren't

3 By the time we arrived at the theater, the play ____.
   a had already started   b already started
   c was already starting

4 When I met Lara I was sure I ____ her somewhere before.
   a saw   b was seeing   c had seen

5 I'd put on a thick jacket and I ____ too warm later.
   a was being   b had been   c was

6 I ____ how the movie would end because I had read the book.
   a had known   b knew   c know

7 He had cut his finger while he ____ the meat.
   a was preparing   b preparing   c had prepared

8 We arrived late to the party, so most of the food ____.
   a was gone   b went   c was going

9 I didn't have any money with me; I ____ my wallet.
   a forget   b forgot   c was forgetting

10 Camilla said she had met Igor while she ____ around Europe.
   a traveled   b was traveling   c had traveled

2 Complete the sentences with the verb pairs. Write one simple past and one past perfect form in each sentence.

say / go   live / move   know / be   meet / know
pass / study   be / lose   finish / leave   be / leave

1 After we _____ our dinner, we _____ the restaurant.
2 The teacher _____ angry because I _____ my work at home.
3 He _____ feeling stressed because he _____ his phone.
4 Jorge _____ all his exams because he _____ hard all year.
5 I _____ Javier once at Laura's house, so I _____ who he was.
6 She _____ in Italy for three years before she _____ to France.
7 Eduardo _____ most of the people at the club because he _____ there before.
8 After I _____ good night, I _____ to bed.

VOCABULARY: Sports and competitions

3 Order the letters to make words that match the definitions.

1 to behave dishonestly in order to achieve something THEAC _____
2 someone who watches people playing sports TRAPECOTS _____
3 to win a point CROSE _____
4 someone who practices a sport very well THELATE _____
5 the person who controls the game FREEREE _____
6 a prize for winning a competition HOTPRY _____

4 Complete the words. Some of the letters are given.

1 She hopes to win a gold m___ ___ ___ ___ at the next Olympics.
2 Our team needs another goal to t___ ___ the score.
3 There was a huge c___ ___ ___ ___ watching last night's game.
4 Don't forget to w___ ___ ___ u___ before you go running.
5 Would you like to t___ ___ ___ p___ ___ ___ in our swimming competition?
6 You can't g___ ___ ___ u___ now. You're nearly at the finishing line!

PRONUNCIATION: 'd/hadn't

5 ▶10.1 Practice saying the sentences. Pay attention to the pronunciation of 'd and hadn't. Listen, check, and repeat.

1 She'd already won the match.
2 He hadn't taken part in the competition.
3 We'd lost both games.
4 They certainly hadn't cheated.
5 We hadn't scored yet.
6 They'd tied in the semifinal.

56

SKILLS 10B

READING: Finding information in a text

Fitness trackers

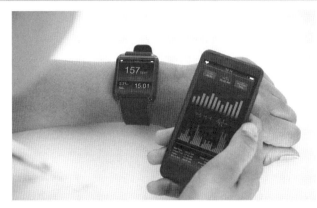

A | Wearable fitness is everywhere you look. There are now hundreds of types of fitness trackers on the market, the simplest of which simply count the number of steps you take in a day. The more sophisticated models record your heartbeat, your food intake, your skin temperature, even how often you snore in your sleep! They allow you to observe and measure details about your own body that previously only doctors were able to see. Which, of course, is fascinating. But apart from providing interest in our lives, are these (often expensive) gadgets worth it? Do they serve any real purpose, other than making a nice profit for a number of companies?

B | Well, it turns out that in a lot of cases they probably do. Not because fitness trackers provide 100% accurate data. (If you try out two different brands of fitness trackers, it's very likely that you'll get two very different step counts over the course of the day.) But because they're always there, often on your wrist, reminding you that you haven't moved or slept enough recently. Turn on your phone and a figure will pop up, telling you how well you're doing. (Some models will even tell you how well your friends are doing!) And that's just what most of us need, a constant reminder that we need to do better.

C | And let's not forget that they're fun. Without a fitness tracker, we may know that we should use our legs more and our wheels less, but we may not actually do anything about it. When we wear a device that rewards us with a "ping" every time we reach our target step count, we are more likely to get off the bus two stops away from work and walk. Daily routines become a sort of game we play with ourselves, and who wouldn't that appeal to?

1 Read the text about gadgets that measure your fitness, then match paragraphs A–C with three of summaries 1–6.

1 A disadvantage of wearable fitness devices. _____
2 What do fitness trackers do? _____
3 The companies that make these fitness devices. _____
4 The enjoyment factor of wearable fitness devices. _____
5 The author's experience of these fitness devices. _____
6 Why wearable fitness devices are useful. _____

2 Read the questions and match them to paragraphs A–C. Then write short answers. There are two questions for each paragraph.

1 What part of the body do you wear some of these devices on? _____
2 What do we all know we should do less of? _____
3 How many different kinds of device are available? _____
4 Where can you look at the information these devices collect? _____
5 What activity do we know we should do more often? _____
6 What can some devices count while you are in bed? _____

3 Complete the sentences with *example*, *for*, *like*, or *such*.

1 We can all get more exercise, _____ instance, by walking rather than driving.
2 With this device daily routines, _____ going upstairs and walking home from the station, can be fun.
3 Everyone can now monitor aspects of their body's behavior, _____ as their heartbeat and temperature.
4 We can find out, for _____, how deeply we're sleeping.

57

10C LANGUAGE

GRAMMAR: Reported speech

1 Complete the sentences with *said* or *told*.

1 She _____ she would call me on the weekend.

2 Nora and Lucia _____ me they had seen you at the gym.

3 She _____ me that Gabriel had gone to the meeting.

4 He _____ that Yolanda would take Lola to the airport.

5 Isaac _____ he would talk to Miguel about the problem.

6 He _____ that Sophia liked her colleagues.

7 Paula _____ me she had met you at the wedding.

8 He _____ me that Lily wasn't coming.

2 Use the prompts to rewrite the sentences in reported speech.

1 "I'll call you from the station."
My sister / tell me / she call me / from the station

_____.

2 "Dad can cook dinner for you and Laura."
My mom / say / Dad cook / dinner for us

_____.

3 "I didn't see Luke in town on Saturday."
He / tell me / he not see / Luke in town on Saturday

_____.

4 "I just bought a new computer."
Maria / say / she buy / a new computer

_____.

5 "We're going to move to France."
He / tell me / they going to move / to France

_____.

6 "I haven't made up my mind."
She / say / she / not make up / her mind

_____.

7 "I'm meeting David on Friday."
Victor / tell me / he meet David / on Friday

_____.

8 "Alba loves going for walks."
He / say / Alba love / going for walks

_____.

VOCABULARY: Parts of the body

3 Match parts of the body a–j with the definitions 1–8.

1 This is in your head and controls how you think. _____

2 This helps your arm bend. _____

3 These are the soft edges of the mouth. _____

4 This helps your leg bend. _____

5 This part of the body contains the heart. _____

6 This is the soft part of the front of the body, above your legs. _____

7 These are the two parts of your body at the tops of your arms. _____

8 This is just above your foot at the bottom of your leg. _____

a shoulders	f lips	
b thumb	g forehead	
c chest	h ankle	
d brain	i elbow	
e stomach	j knee	

4 Complete the words. The first letters are given.

1 After running, the m___ ___ ___ ___ ___ ___ in my legs were tired.

2 She'd broken a b___ ___ ___ in her foot and couldn't walk.

3 Anna was wearing a pretty scarf around her n___ ___ ___.

4 A healthy diet and regular exercise are good for your h___ ___ ___ ___ .

5 He was wearing sandals, so I could see his t___ ___ ___.

6 After a few days in the sun, her s___ ___ ___ was really brown.

7 Why is she pointing a f___ ___ ___ ___ ___ at me?

8 Victor has an expensive-looking watch on his left w___ ___ ___ ___.

PRONUNCIATION: Weak form of *that*

5 ▶10.2 Listen to the sentences. Is *that* strong (S) or weak (W)? Listen, check, and repeat.

1 Monica said that she was leaving. _____

2 Is that your cousin over there? _____

3 That's not what I said! _____

4 Kevin told me that I was wrong. _____

5 Pam said that the party started at eight. _____

6 Could you give me that book, please? _____

7 Beatriz told Clara that she was angry. _____

8 Sara likes the blue bike, but I like that one. _____

58

SKILLS 10D

SPEAKING: Making inquiries

1 ▶10.3 Gabriella is a guest at an expensive hotel. Listen to her conversation with the receptionist. Are the statements true (T) or false (F)?

1 Gabriella didn't know that the hotel had a fitness center. ____
2 The exercise room has a lot of equipment that guests can use. ____
3 Gabriella wants someone to show her the gym. ____
4 Guests don't have to pay to use the swimming pool. ____
5 The swimming pool closes at night. ____
6 The receptionist will send an extra towel to Gabriella's room. ____

2 ▶10.3 Listen again. You will hear seven of these phrases. Write G (Gabriella) or R (receptionist).

a Can I help you? ____
b Could you give me some information about ..., please? ____
c Just one more thing. ____
d Excuse me, could you tell me ...? ____
e I'd also like to ask about ... ____
f Does that sound OK? ____
g I was told ... Is that true? ... ____
h Is there anything else... ? ____
i Should I ...? ____
j Can I just double check? Do you ...? ____
k Would you like me to ...? ____
l Could I speak to someone about ...? ____
m I was hoping you could help me. ____

3 Put the phrases from exercise 2 into the correct categories.

1 starting an inquiry politely ___ ___ ___ ___
2 asking for additional information ___ ___ ___ ___
3 being helpful ___ ___ ___

4 ▶10.4 Use the phrases in exercise 2 to complete these conversations. There may be more than one possible answer. Then listen and say the missing part aloud.

1 **In a sports store**

A Good morning. Can I help you?
B Hello. ¹_____ sneakers, please? I'm looking for a pair for long-distance running.
A Yes, we have several running shoes. Can I bring some for you to try on?
B That would be great, thanks. ²_____ waterproof jackets.
A We don't have any available at the moment, but here's a catalog. You can order them online. Does that sound OK?

2 **At the gym**

A Excuse me, can I take Pilates classes here?
B Yes, we have several teachers. ³_____ give you a list?
A Great, thanks.
B You can call them to arrange a time. ⁴_____?
A Yes, perfect, thanks.
B Here's the list. ⁵_____?
A No, that's everything. Thanks for your help.

59

10 REVIEW and PRACTICE

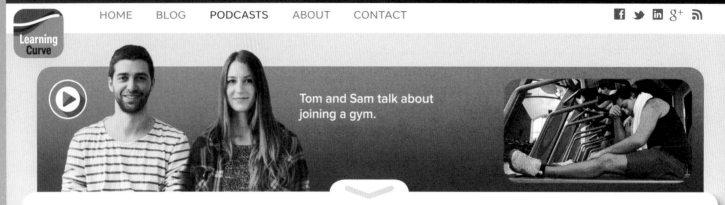

LISTENING

1 ▶ 10.5 Listen to the podcast. Check (✓) the parts of the body that are mentioned.

- a foot ____
- b neck ____
- c muscle ____
- d ankle ____
- e wrist ____
- f stomach ____
- g shoulder ____
- h bone ____
- i heart ____
- j knee ____

2 ▶ 10.5 Listen again. Choose the correct options to complete the sentences.

1. How long has Harry been going to the sports center?
   a about one year
   b about two years
   c about five years
2. For his height, Harry
   a weighs too little.
   b weighs the right amount.
   c weighs too much.
3. Harry wants a workout that's good for his
   a stomach.
   b muscles.
   c heart.
4. Harry says that he
   a has always been active.
   b has never gotten much exercise.
   c has never injured himself.
5. Harry had to have an operation when he was
   a eight.
   b eleven.
   c twenty.
6. What happened while Harry was skiing?
   a He injured his leg.
   b He damaged part of his arm.
   c He caused a serious accident.

READING

1 Read the blog about sports injuries. Choose the best summary.

a Peter didn't prepare enough for his run and, because of his injury, he will never be able to run again.
b Peter hadn't realized there was a problem with his ankle and made things worse by getting more exercise.
c Peter wasn't used to getting much exercise, and hurt his ankle badly soon after starting his run.

2 Choose the correct options to complete the sentences.

1. According to Peter, after a sports injury you feel
   a upset and annoyed.
   b surprised and frightened.
   c tired and embarrassed.
2. Peter hurt his ankle
   a when he got up one day.
   b while he was running.
   c when he was preparing to run.
3. Peter's doctor told him
   a to stop running for a few weeks.
   b to run shorter distances.
   c to stop running completely.
4. Peter had
   a had a few injuries in the past.
   b never injured himself before.
   c only recently started running.
5. Peter says that stress
   a makes it take longer to recover from injury.
   b is hard for most people to control.
   c can make it difficult for him to run.
6. Peter says that he
   a thought his ankle would never get better.
   b was impatient to recover as quickly as possible.
   c did what his doctor had told him to do.

REVIEW and PRACTICE 10

HOME   **BLOG**   PODCASTS   ABOUT   CONTACT

Guest blogger Kate gets some advice on recovering from sports injuries.

How I got back on track

We all know we should get plenty of exercise and many of us have a favorite sport or activity. But what happens if you suffer an injury and can't practice the sport you love? How do you cope with it, and how do you recover from it? Peter Jackson, sports coach and runner, told us about his experience of being injured.

It's tough. You feel so many negative emotions. You're angry because you can't practice your sport. You feel disappointed because your body has failed you. And you're bored because you can't do what you want to do!

One morning last year I got up and noticed a problem with my right ankle. It was a slight pain at first and I thought it would go away. I'd done a long run the day before—a few miles more than usual—and thought maybe that was the reason. Anyway, I went running, as usual. I'd done everything correctly to prepare. I'd put a bandage on for support and, of course, I'd warmed up before starting.

But as I ran, the pain got worse and worse and, after three miles, I had to give up and go home. The next day, I saw my doctor who told me that I'd injured my ankle badly and that I would have to rest it for four to six weeks; that meant no running at all! It was kind of a shock. Until that point, I'd run every day for the previous four or five years, with no problems. Suddenly, I had to learn new habits. Most importantly, I had to start listening to my body, and it was telling me to rest.

Of course, at first I was very stressed by not being able to run, but I learned to manage that. It's often said that stress is caused by the feeling that we can't control a situation, and stress stops the body from getting better. So the first thing I had to understand was that I was in control because I was helping myself get better. I couldn't take part in running any more, but by resting my ankle and doing the exercises that the doctor had shown me, I was taking part in my recovery. I learned to be patient, to accept that it takes time to get better and, above all, I learned to be positive and to believe that I would recover.

UNIT 11 At home

GRAMMAR: -ing/infinitive verb patterns

1 Choose the correct options to complete the sentences.

1 I have arranged ____ Rita this evening.
   a meeting   b to meet
2 Did you finish ____ your bedroom yet?
   a decorating   b to decorate
3 Frankie can't stand ____ early.
   a getting up   b to get up
4 The company is planning ____ its factory in Ohio.
   a closing   b to close
5 Oh no! I forgot ____ my passport!
   a bringing   b to bring
6 Would you mind ____ dinner tonight?
   a cooking   b to cook
7 Gary hopes ____ a place on the team.
   a getting   b to get
8 Do you feel like ____ to the beach today?
   a going   b to go
9 I can't imagine ____ a marathon!
   a running   b to run
10 Unfortunately, I can't afford ____ a vacation this year.
   a taking   b to take

2 Complete the text with the correct form of the verbs in the box.

| get | move | tell | play |
| visit | stay | hang out | pay |

Last year, I decided ¹____ to another city. I was bored with my job, and I wanted a change. I'm the kind of person that hates ²____ in the same place for too long. Luckily, I managed ³____ a new job fairly quickly. My new company even offered ⁴____ my rent for three months while I looked for a place to buy. The only problem was my great friend, Stan. He kept ⁵____ me that I would be lonely and that I'd miss ⁶____ with him and our other friends. I did feel sorry about leaving Stan, but I knew I'd make new friends quickly. I love ⁷____ soccer and joining a team is always a good way to meet people. However, I promised ⁸____ Stan as often as I could, and I've kept my promise.

VOCABULARY: Household items

3 Order the letters to make words that match the descriptions.

1 It keeps you warm in bed. FMCOETRRO   _____
2 You turn it on and water comes out. TFUACE   _____
3 You put dirty clothes in it. GASWNHI CHANMIE   _____
4 You keep your clothes in it.
  THESC FO REWARDS   _____
5 They are made of thin material and go on a bed. THESES   _____
6 It keeps your house warm.
  ANCTLER THIGANE   _____

4 Complete the crossword puzzle.

Across
3 Put the _____ on the sofa.
5 I sleep best with a soft _____ under my head.
8 Pia had a _____ full of beautiful clothes.
9 I washed my hands in the bathroom _____.

Down
1 A _____ is a small carpet.
2 All the dirty dishes need to go in the _____.
4 It was cold, so we put an extra _____ on the bed.
6 Is the _____ hot enough yet to do my shirt?
7 The cake must be done, so take it out of the _____.

PRONUNCIATION: Sentence stress

5 ▶11.1 Listen to these sentences and repeat them. Pay attention to the way *to* is pronounced.

1 Gary can't afford to buy a new laptop.
2 The children enjoy playing in the park.
3 We plan to meet our friends at eight.
4 I don't feel like going to the movies.
5 I forgot to lock the door.
6 Silvia doesn't want to come with us.

SKILLS 11B

LISTENING: Understanding and interpreting information

1 ▶11.2 Read the sentences and look at the underlined words. Think about other words the speakers might use. Then listen to the conversation. Are the sentences true (T) or false (F)?

1 Johnny is <u>extremely tired</u> after doing the housework. _____
2 Johnny has <u>cleaned</u> the kitchen floor. _____
3 Marta says Johnny's roommates will be <u>very pleased</u> with him. _____
4 As part of Marta and Sara's <u>agreement</u>, Marta cleans the house. _____
5 Marta tells Johnny she <u>hates</u> cleaning. _____
6 Marta's roommate, Sara, <u>really likes</u> food. _____
7 Marta says the meals she cooks are <u>very good</u>. _____
8 Marta says she spends <u>a lot of time</u> deciding what to cook. _____

2 ▶11.2 Listen again and check and write the actual words the speakers use.

1 extremely tired _____
2 cleaned _____
3 very pleased _____
4 agreement _____
5 hates _____
6 really likes _____
7 very good _____
8 a lot of time _____

3 Read the short conversations. Write the words that the speakers don't say.

1 A She was angry.
  B No, she wasn't. _____
2 A Do you think Maria's happy at work?
  B Not so sure about that! _____
3 A What's wrong?
  B Computer's not working! _____
4 A You look really stressed.
  B Yes! Big problem with the plans for Saturday! _____
5 A Sara doesn't like cooking, I'm guessing?
  B No, hates it! _____

4 Match a–e with missing words 1–5 in exercise 3.

a pronouns _____
b articles _____
c *be* and auxiliary verbs _____
d *There is/are* _____
e avoid repeating words _____

5 Match the two parts of the sentences.

1 We'll need to set _____
2 Tom said he was mopping _____
3 Could you hang out _____
4 I completely forgot to water _____
5 After we finished eating, we loaded _____
6 Ella got up and had breakfast, then made _____
7 He dropped some food and had to vacuum _____
8 Don't forget to take out _____

a the plants in the garden.
b these clothes to dry, please?
c the trash, please.
d the carpet.
e the dishwasher.
f the bathroom floor when I called.
g her bed.
h the dinner table for six people.

63

11C LANGUAGE

GRAMMAR: Articles

1 Match the two parts of the sentences.

1 I would really love a ____
2 Paul said he would like an ____
3 I think I will enjoy the ____
4 We could have ____
5 Esther talked a lot about ____
6 Laura explained how ____
7 Rick told me about an ____
8 Maria described a ____

a book you told us about.
b to get to Bill's house.
c drink.
d village in China.
e old friend who was a musician.
f orange.
g politics.
h breakfast before we go.

2 Complete the sentences with the correct article or – (no article).

1 Vivian sees the doctor twice _____ year.
2 We went to _____ amazing concert last night.
3 I'm a little scared of _____ dogs.
4 She gave _____ taxi driver a big tip.
5 Patsy has to go to _____ hospital tomorrow.
6 I usually have sandwiches for _____ lunch.
7 _____ Monday is the first day of the working week.
8 They have to go to _____ bank before it closes.
9 What's _____ name of Pete's girlfriend?
10 My sister is _____ engineer.

3 Read the review and choose the correct sequence of articles, A, B, or C.

> ### "Spectacles" review *****
>
> This week we're reviewing Spectacles, ¹____ pair of sunglasses that can take ²____ videos. ³____ product is made by ⁴____ video and messaging app, Snapchat. ⁵____ videos are ⁶____ unusual shape: they're round, similar to human vision. Spectacles' 10-second video clips are sent via Bluetooth to users' smartphones.
>
> | | | | | | |
> |---|---|---|---|---|---|
> | **A** 1 – | 2 – | 3 – | 4 the | 5 – | 6 a |
> | **B** 1 a | 2 – | 3 The | 4 the | 5 The | 6 an |
> | **C** 1 a | 2 the | 3 The | 4 – | 5 The | 6 the |

VOCABULARY: Words to describe materials and clothes

4 Complete the sentences with the words in the box.

> silk   fur   casual   wood   wool   metal

1 I'm an animal lover, so I don't wear _____ coats.
2 You need to polish _____ jewelry to make it shine.
3 It's best to wash _____ shirts by hand.
4 We gave Helga an unusual _____ ring for her birthday.
5 In winter, I wear a _____ sweater to keep warm.
6 Joe packed some _____ clothes for his vacation.

5 Complete the words.

1 My sister is a vegetarian and won't even buy l__ __ __ __ __ __ shoes.
2 You should wear f__ __ __ __ __ clothes for an interview.
3 In summer Felipe prefers short-sleeved c__ __ __ __ __ shirts.
4 We aren't allowed to wear d__ __ __ __ jeans to work.
5 Are these pants too t__ __ __ __? I think I need a larger size.
6 She didn't buy the skirt with flowers on it because she wanted something p__ __ __ __.

PRONUNCIATION: the

6 ▶ 11.3 Listen and circle the pronunciation of *the* that you hear. Listen, check, and repeat.

1	We need to take **the** early train.	/ðə/	/ði/
2	Where are all **the** other people?	/ðə/	/ði/
3	What time does **the** concert start?	/ðə/	/ði/
4	Should we meet at **the** usual place?	/ðə/	/ði/
5	Don't forget to bring **the** tickets.	/ðə/	/ði/
6	His house is painted pink on **the** outside.	/ðə/	/ði/
7	How did you do on **the** exam?	/ðə/	/ði/
8	I spilled juice on **the** carpet.	/ðə/	/ði/

SKILLS 11D

WRITING: Making writing interesting

1 Read David's description of his friend's house and complete it with the words in the box.

> so (x 2)   because   but   although   however   and   also   as well

Michael's house

My friend Michael lives with his parents in a big modern house just outside the city. I think it's an excellent place to live ¹_____ it's really peaceful there, ²_____ it's still easy to get to the city on the bus.

Michael's mom is an excellent gardener, and they have a gorgeous yard with lots of flowers. It ³_____ has a large swimming pool, where we often hang out on the weekends.

⁴_____ the rooms in Michael's house are spacious, they're still very comfortable. In Michael's room, there's an old leather sofa ⁵_____ lots of soft red velvet cushions. There's a lovely thick rug, ⁶_____.

All the rooms have big windows ⁷_____ they're bright and airy. ⁸_____, most of them have thick, black blinds, ⁹_____ you can make the rooms dark if you want to. That's especially useful in the living room, where we often watch movies.

2 Order the adjectives to complete the sentences.

1. He owns a(n) _____ bed. (huge/amazing/square)
2. Her bedroom has _____ curtains. (pale green/silk/fashionable)
3. My house contains a _____ living area. (spacious/modern)
4. Their home is full of _____ furniture. (old/oak/beautiful)
5. She uses _____ sheets on the beds. (Egyptian/white/cotton)
6. I don't like the _____ window frames. (horrible/plastic/modern)
7. On the table there is a _____ vase. (Chinese/large/round)
8. The dining room has a _____ carpet. (blue/gorgeous)

3 Find these words in the text and match them with synonyms a–d.

1. spacious   ____
2. gorgeous   ____
3. hang out   ____
4. get to   ____

a. spend time
b. reach
c. large
d. beautiful

4 Find two examples in the text of *where* and an example of what you can do there. Then complete 1–4 with your own ideas.

1. Greg's house has a gorgeous long yard, where _____.

2. Anna's cottage has an an old red living room, where _____.

3. Peter's apartment has an enormous square balcony, where _____.

4. There is a wonderful modern kitchen, where _____.

5 Write a description of a home you like.

- Use adjectives in the correct order.
- Use synonyms to avoid repeating words.
- Use linkers to give reasons and results (*so, because, that's why*), to contrast information (*but, although, however*) or add information (*and, also, too, as well*).
- Include a sentence with *where* and what you can do in a particular place.

65

11 REVIEW and PRACTICE

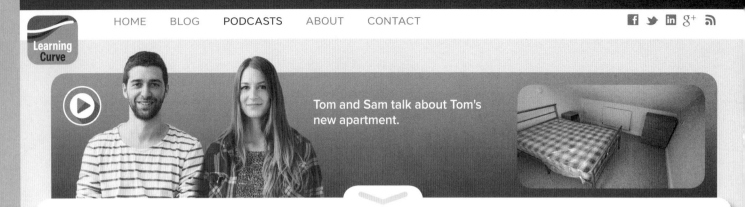

Tom and Sam talk about Tom's new apartment.

LISTENING

1 ▶ 11.4 Listen to the podcast. Number these things in the order Tom mentions them.

a closet _____
b sofa _____
c freezer _____
d central heating _____
e kitchen _____
f comforter _____
g refrigerator _____
h chest of drawers _____

2 ▶ 11.4 Listen again. Is each statement correct (Yes) or incorrect (No)?

	Yes	No
1 Tom has been in his new home for less than a month.	☐	☐
2 Tom moved in on the coldest day of the year.	☐	☐
3 Tom had to go to bed early to keep warm.	☐	☐
4 Tom was pleased the central heating was soon fixed.	☐	☐
5 Tom hasn't had time to put his clothes in the closet.	☐	☐
6 At the moment, Tom doesn't mind not having a freezer.	☐	☐
7 Tom would prefer different wallpaper in his new home.	☐	☐
8 Tom is confident that Sam will really like his apartment.	☐	☐

READING

1 Read the blog about house-sharing. Check (✓) the correct sentences, according to the information in the blog.

1 Real estate prices are rising, so more people share houses today than ever before. _____
2 People often need to share houses or apartments, but there can be problems. _____
3 You need to make sure your new roommate can afford to live there. _____
4 Feelings are important, but you can take practical steps to make sharing a house or apartment successful. _____
5 If you can't share with someone you know, you should at least meet the person before you move in together. _____
6 You should make a list of important things about where you are going to live. _____

2 Are the sentences true (T), false (F), or isn't there enough information to decide (N)?

1 Many people have bad experiences with roommates. _____
2 Mollie's roommate didn't know how to use their washing machine. _____
3 Jamie liked his roommate's snake. _____
4 A lot of people move into houses or apartments they can't really afford. _____
5 Becky's roommate was often late paying her rent. _____
6 It doesn't matter why someone left the last place they lived. _____
7 Daniel didn't like the type of music his roommates played. _____
8 If you don't feel comfortable with someone, you should find out where they lived before. _____
9 Websites can be a good place to find house-sharing opportunities. _____
10 At a speed housemating event, you can immediately find out basic information about people. _____

REVIEW and PRACTICE 11

HOME　BLOG　PODCASTS　ABOUT　CONTACT

Guest blogger Penny explains how to find the perfect housemate.

The highs and lows of house-sharing

You want to leave home, but you can't afford your own apartment or house. What do you do? Sharing accommodations with other people in the same situation is the obvious answer. But how do you find those people, and how do you know you will get along with them? The Internet is full of horror stories, and here are a few of them!

"One of my roommates never changed his sheets," says 21-year-old Mollie Goodman. "Eventually the whole house started to smell!" 23-year-old Jamie King also had bad experiences. "In one place I lived, this guy moved in and brought a huge snake with him. Even worse, he filled the freezer with dead mice to feed it!"

Of course, money's another issue. You might be embarrassed to ask someone how they plan to pay the rent, but you don't want to end up like Becky. Her roommate claimed to be an actor, but the truth was that she was usually out of work. Not only did she rarely pay her rent on time, she also thought it was OK to use Becky's shampoo, drink her milk, and even "borrow" her clothes (without asking, of course!).

If you're the person moving into a house or apartment, find out why the last person left. Maybe, like Daniel Mills, 24, it was because the others were all in a band together, and rehearsed at home! "I never got a moment's peace; it was terrible!" he says. "If you're the one with a spare room, *always* ask for references from the people they lived with before. And listen to your heart. If you have a bad feeling about someone, just walk away. But listen to your head as well. Even if someone seems great, get an agreement in writing."

Most of us would prefer to live with someone we know, but that's not always possible, especially when you move to a new city. Online house-sharing sites are a good place to start. But one thing everyone agrees on is that you must meet the people you're going to live with face to face before you move in. Because this can take a lot of time, "speed housemating" events are becoming more and more popular. At these events people with rooms can meet people who want to rent. Everyone wears a sticker showing their budget and where they want to live. It's like speed dating, but with a front door key thrown in!

UNIT 12 People and relationships

12A — LANGUAGE

GRAMMAR: Defining relative clauses

1 Choose the correct options to complete the sentences.

1 Did you see the photo *who / that or - / where* I posted yesterday?

2 Is that the neighbor *who / - / where* bake the cake for your birthday?

3 That building on the left is the office *that / who / where* I used to work.

4 The woman *where / who / -* usually cuts my hair has left.

5 He loves playing sports *where / that or - / who* he hasn't tried before.

6 She told me about a restaurant *that / where / who* they make really good vegetarian food.

7 We could meet at that French café—the one *that or - / where / who* you mentioned earlier.

8 For people *- / who / where* prefer peace and quiet, this hotel is perfect.

9 Is she the girl *that or - / where / what* you were telling me about?

10 This is the room *that / who / where* most of the meetings take place.

2 Combine the two sentences using a relative pronoun.

1 That's the hotel. We stayed there in May.

_____

2 I lost the necklace. Marta gave it to me for my birthday.

_____

3 Did you hear the joke? Alan told it earlier.

_____

4 She shouted to the boy. He had dropped his phone.

_____

5 This is the bus. It goes to Chicago.

_____

6 Are they going to the restaurant? It opened last month.

_____

VOCABULARY: Relationships

3 Order the letters to make words that match the definitions.

1 someone who you share a house or apartment with OOMRETAM _____

2 a person or organization that gives people work REPLOYME _____

3 someone who hates another person and tries to harm them MEENY _____

4 someone that you work with GLOECLEAU _____

5 someone that you live near to HENIGROB _____

6 a man who is getting married or just got married MOROG _____

7 someone who you own a company with SUBISSEN TRAPERN _____

8 the brother of your husband or wife, or your sister's husband ROBERTH-NI-WAL _____

4 Complete the words. Some letters are given.

1 My father left when we were little, so my mother was a s___ ___ ___ ___ ___ parent.

2 My mother remarried and had a daughter, so I have a s___ ___ ___ ___ ___ ___ ___ ___ ___.

3 She has one cousin living near her, but no other r___ ___ ___ ___ ___ ___ ___.

4 I don't have brothers or sisters; I'm an o___ ___ ___ child.

5 Sarah doesn't get along with her husband's parents, but I love my i___ -l___ ___ ___.

6 My aunts and uncles all have children, so I have lots of c___ ___ ___ ___ ___ ___.

7 I didn't like the last guy I worked for, but my new b___ ___ ___ is great.

8 Ted's g___ ___ ___ ___ ___ ___ ___ ___ ___ came to the nightclub; they've been going out for six months.

PRONUNCIATION: Sentence stress

5 ▶ 12.1 Look at the relative pronouns *who*, *which*, and *where*. Are they stressed (S) or unstressed (U)? Listen, check, and repeat.

1 Who did you speak to? **S U**

2 That's the town where he grew up. **S U**

3 She must be the woman who works here. **S U**

4 Where are the instructions? **S U**

5 Did she say which flight she was taking? **S U**

6 Which jacket looks better with these pants? **S U**

SKILLS 12B

READING: Interpreting data

A

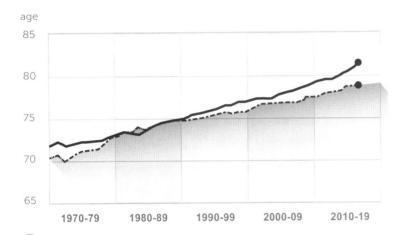

B

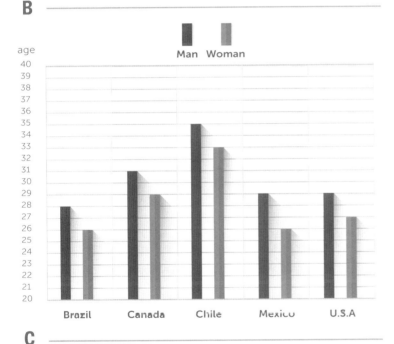

C

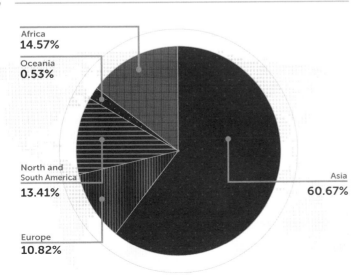

1 Match the information in Graphs A–C with three of 1–6.

1. World population by continent. ____
2. Average temperatures by continent. ____
3. Male and female life expectancy. ____
4. Average age of first marriage. ____
5. U.K. and U.S. population change. ____
6. Life expectancy in the U.S. and U.K. ____

2 According to Graphs A–C, are these statements true (T) or false (F)?

1. Life expectancy in the U.S. rose by more than five years from 1990 to 2010. ____
2. In 1980, life expectancy for both U.K. and U.S. citizens was still less than 75. ____
3. The difference between life expectancy in the U.K. and the U.S. increased from 1990 to 2010. ____
4. The average age difference between men and women for their first marriage is two years everywhere except Canada. ____
5. Chilean people are older at the time of their first marriage than other nationalities on this chart. ____
6. Brazilian women are the same age as women from the U.S. when they get married for the first time. ____
7. Asia has the highest population of any continent. ____
8. The population of Africa is about 3% larger than that of North and South America. ____
9. Fewer people live in North and South America than in Europe. ____

3 Choose the correct options to complete this summary of Graph A.

Graph A shows that from 1970 to 2012, U.K. citizens almost always lived slightly ¹*longer / shorter* lives than U.S. citizens. Both groups have ²*increased / decreased* their life expectancy by ³*around / at least* 10 years during the period shown. From 1970 to 1979, life expectancy for U.S. citizens increased by ⁴*at least / nearly* five years. From 1975 to 1995, data for the U.K. and the U.S. were ⁵*not at all / roughly* similar. However, for a brief time around 1980, the life expectancy of U.S. citizens was just ⁶*over / under* that of people in the U.K. By 1982, life expectancy in both the U.S. and the U.K. had reached ⁷*at least / almost* 75. By 2012, the average person in the U.K. could expect to live to ⁸*at least / nearly* 80.

12C LANGUAGE

GRAMMAR: Uses of the *-ing* form and the infinitive

1 Choose the correct options to complete the sentences.

1 I was disappointed about ____ the exam.
   a to fail   b failing

2 Before ____, maybe we should have something to eat.
   a to leave   b leaving

3 She just left the office ____ some lunch.
   a getting   b to get

4 ____ is the best form of exercise.
   a To walk   b Walking

5 I agree there's a problem, although I think it's unfair ____ Jim.
   a blaming   b to blame

6 It's not expensive ____ on a camping trip.
   a going   b to go

7 It was impossible not ____ her my secret!
   a to tell   b telling

8 ____ time with friends is so important.
   a Spending   b To spend

9 Not ____ meat can be difficult in some countries.
   a to eat   b eating

2 Complete the sentences with the verbs in the box. Use each verb twice, once in the *-ing* form and once in the infinitive.

> earn   see   discuss   eat   speak

1 She was too afraid _____ to her boss about the situation.

2 We were both hungry, so we went home _____.

3 _____ a lot of money is hard work.

4 After _____ the matter, we came to a decision.

5 Are you interested in _____ a movie this evening?

6 _____ to a room of two hundred people is terrifying.

7 I'd be interested _____ her face when she hears the news!

8 I was delighted _____ a little extra money.

9 Fernando and I met _____ the problem.

10 _____ a lot of sugar is bad for your health.

VOCABULARY: Relationship verbs

3 Choose the correct options to complete the sentences.

1 I met a really nice girl on Saturday and thought I might ____ her **out**.
   a keep   b ask   c go

2 Karla and Javier ended their relationship, but ____ **back together** last month.
   a got   b fell   c broke

3 Did you know that Bernie and Karen are ____ **married** next year?
   a making   b getting   c going

4 Joe and Eve used to go ____ **together**, but they broke up.
   a on   b in   c out

5 Connie is **going on** a ____ tonight with a guy she met at work.
   a date   b marriage   c break

6 I've known Pablo for ten years. We ____ **friends** when we lived in Mexico City.
   a became   b got   c went

4 Complete the sentences.

1 Although Laura and I live in different countries, we manage to stay in _____.

2 They met and _____ in love while they were in college.

3 We have similar interests and opinions. In general, we _____ a lot in common.

4 Nancy is single again. She broke _____ with her boyfriend a week ago.

5 Alejandro seems interesting. I'd like to _____ to know him better.

6 Isabella's great! I've always gotten _____ really well with her.

PRONUNCIATION: Word stress

5 ▶ 12.2 Match 1–8 with stress patterns a–e. Listen, check and repeat.

1 important ____   a ○ o
2 colleague ____   b o ○
3 impossible ____   c o ○ o
4 except ____   d ○ o o
5 technology ____   e o ○ o o
6 better ____
7 afraid ____
8 probably ____

SKILLS 12D

SPEAKING: Saying thanks

1 ▶12.3 Listen to the conversation between Anna and Tim. Which four of these phrases do they use? Number them 1–4 in the order that you hear them.

a Thanks a lot. _____
b That's very nice of you. _____
c Thanks a million. _____
d Thanks. _____
e Thank you so much. _____
f Thanks very much. _____
g I can't thank you enough. _____
h I really appreciate it. _____
i I'm very grateful to you. _____

2 Read the four phrases from the conversation. Match them to the different ways of responding modestly.

1 Oh, I'm glad you like it. It's a really easy recipe. _____ _____
2 Not at all. It would be a lot of fun. _____
3 It's nothing, really! _____
4 Well, to be honest, not many other people entered. _____

   a saying you are pleased
   b saying something isn't difficult
   c saying something is not as good as the other person thinks
   d saying you would enjoy doing something
   e saying something is only a small thing

3 ▶12.4 Listen to five people speaking. Choose the most appropriate response.

1 That's very nice of you. / Thanks.
2 Thanks a lot. / I'm very grateful to you.
3 Thanks very much. / I really appreciate it.
4 Thanks a lot. / I can't thank you enough.
5 I can't thank you enough. / Thanks a million.

4 ▶12.5 Listen to four people thanking, congratulating or complimenting you. Use your own ideas to respond modestly.

1 You're welcome. _____.
2 I'm glad you think so, but _____.
3 No problem. _____.
4 Thanks. _____.

5 ▶12.6 Listen to some possible answers to exercise 4.

71

12 REVIEW and PRACTICE

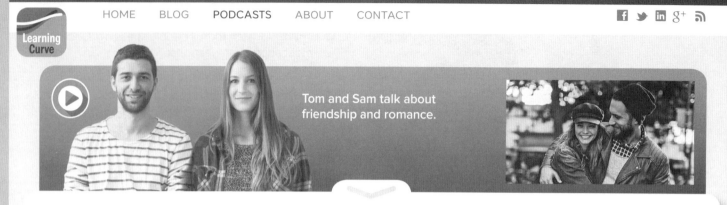

LISTENING

1 ▶ 12.7 Listen to the podcast. Are the statements true (T) or false (F), according to the speaker?

1 Sophie didn't get along with Marco to begin with. _____
2 Friendships can become romantic relationships. _____
3 What makes a good friend also makes a good partner. _____

2 ▶ 12.7 Listen again. Choose the correct options to complete the sentences.

1 Sophie met Marco in
   a school.
   b college.
   c work.
2 When they were in college, they
   a rarely spoke to each other.
   b never spoke to each other.
   c were in contact with each other.
3 In New York, Sophie and Marco fell in love
   a over a period of time.
   b immediately.
   c with other people.
4 Sophie says that when two people start going out together, they
   a can be too honest with each other.
   b usually feel better about themselves.
   c often try to appear better than they are.
5 When Sophie started going out with Marco, she
   a already knew his personality.
   b didn't really like it.
   c found out new things about him.
6 Sophie says that people often choose a partner because
   a they have lots in common.
   b of their appearance.
   c of their honesty.
7 She says that finding someone physically attractive
   a may not be enough in a relationship.
   b is often bad for a relationship.
   c is usually good for a relationship.

READING

1 Read the blog about five people's problems. Complete 1–5 with the words in the box. There are three extra words.

> classmate   partners   boss   roommate
> neighbors   colleagues   relative   girlfriend

2 Match the advice in 1–8 with problems A–E.

1 You should try to get to know the people you work with. _____
2 It's not a good idea to communicate with this person. _____
3 You might meet someone special through your friends. _____
4 You have to remember that most people are busy. _____
5 There's not much you can do to change this situation. _____
6 Think of ways to start up a conversation with them. _____
7 Most people experience this at some point in their life. _____
8 You're unlikely to make friends at work if you're the boss. _____

REVIEW and PRACTICE 12

HOME BLOG PODCASTS ABOUT CONTACT

Tom and Sam give some advice about readers' problems.

You have your say

We've learned so much about other people through writing this blog. Since this is our last one, we've invited our readers to write in with their problems to see if we can give them some advice.

A *We just moved to a new town. No one talks to us or shows any interest, and we feel we're not welcome. Can you help?*

It's not that your ¹_____ dislike you–they're just going on with their lives, going to work, seeing their friends, etc., and that doesn't leave much time for you! Why not invent a reason to talk to them? Ask when the next garbage pick-up is, or which items you can recycle. People generally like to be helpful and the conversation might lead to other things.

B *I have a small company and my employees get along well. The problem is that they treat me differently. They never talk to me during their breaks or ask me to go out with them.*

To be honest, you probably just have to accept it. Your employees may respect you, even like you, but you're not their friend–you're their ²_____ and you have a different relationship with them. If you're short of friends, you need to look in other places.

C *I broke up with my ³_____ last week and it's all I can think about. I'm OK at work, but at home I don't know what to do with myself. I feel so sad and lonely.*

You probably won't like this, but you have to stop thinking about her. The relationship's over—she's made that clear. Get out and meet new people and you'll stop thinking about her.

D *I'm a single parent. I have great friends, but they're all getting married or have girlfriends or boyfriends, and I'm always the lonely guy at the party. Any ideas?*

So your friends all have ⁴_____. It happens to everyone after a certain age. But why aren't they introducing you to their single friends? Why not suggest it? After all, if you get along with them, there's a good chance you'll get along with their friends. One of them may be your future partner!

E *I moved here recently for a new job, and I don't know anyone. I'm single, and I'm spending all my time alone. I'd love to make friends, but I'm shy.*

Come on, don't wait for people to come to you! What about those new ⁵_____? Use your coffee breaks to get to know them. You'll soon find you have things in common and the next thing you know, you'll be watching movies together!

73

WRITING PRACTICE

WRITING: Writing an essay

1 Read the essay about eating meat and put paragraphs A–E in order. Use the linkers to help you (*First, The second reason, Finally, In conclusion*).

A ____   B ____   C ____   D ____   E ____

Should humans stop eating meat?

A   The second reason is the environment. Raising animals for food produces gases that increase global warming. In addition, the animals need to be given huge amounts of water and grain. Also, some studies say that we would need twenty times less land to feed people instead of animals.

B   People have been eating meat for thousands of years, and they seem to love it. According to one report, the average American eats around 25 kilos of beef, 27 kilos of chicken and 22 kilos of pork in a year. But is it a good idea to go on like this? I don't believe that it is.

C   In conclusion, I realize that many people love eating meat, but I would say that vegetarian food can be just as tasty. In any case, our world is changing. We are facing serious problems of climate change, obesity, and disease, and, in my opinion, it's time for us to change too—before it's too late.

D   First, there's the question of the animals themselves. We go to a supermarket and buy a piece of meat in a package, but that meat was once a little lamb or a cute calf. Personally, I love all animals and I don't want to eat them!

E   Finally, there is more and more evidence that eating fruit and vegetables is healthy and eating too much meat is not. I'm worried that diseases such as diabetes and heart disease are becoming more common because many people eat too much, and in particular too much meat.

2 The author talks about three main issues: protecting animals (A), the environment (E), and our health (H). Write the correct letter next to the arguments she uses.

1 There would be more food for people if we didn't eat meat. ____
2 A vegetarian diet is better for people than eating meat. ____
3 We don't think about animals enough when we eat them. ____
4 Eating meat may be increasing diseases. ____
5 The gas from keeping animals leads to global warming. ____
6 Obesity is a serious problem. ____

3 Read the opinions about "meat-free Monday"–the idea that you should have one day a week without meat. Complete them with the words in the box, then say if each one is for (F) or against (A) meat-free Monday.

> think   delighted   worried   say   bad   opinion   personally   good

1 In my _____, we need meat to stay strong and healthy.
2 _____, I feel much healthier when I don't eat meat.
3 It's always a _____ idea to eat more vegetables.
4 I _____ our bodies and teeth are designed to eat meat.
5 I'm _____ farmers would suffer.
6 I would _____ that vegetarian food can be as tasty as meat.
7 I'm _____ more people are giving up meat because I love animals.
8 It's a _____ idea to stop eating meat because it makes us stronger.

4 Write an essay on the subject "Everyone should have a meat-free Monday."

- You can use ideas from exercise 3 or your own ideas.
- Organize your ideas into five paragraphs: introduction, reasons 1–3, conclusion.
- Give examples and evidence to support your reasons.
- Use the linkers from exercise 1.

WRITING PRACTICE

WRITING: Writing a formal e-mail

1 Read Ben's formal e-mail complaining about his gym classes. What is the correct order of the paragraphs?

1 _____ 2 _____ 3 _____

To: info@gymsforall.com

Subject: Exercise classes

[1]*Dear Sir/Madam:*

A

In recent weeks, a large number of classes [2]*have been canceled* without notice. [3]*In addition to this*, several of the teachers appear to be extremely inexperienced, leading to a real risk of injury.

B

In my opinion, all exercise instructors should [4]*be checked* regularly to [5]*ensure* that [6]*they are* teaching to the highest standards. Would you please let me know as soon as possible how you intend to improve this unsatisfactory situation.

C

[7]*I am writing* [8]*with regard to* the standard of the exercise classes at your gym, which I believe has reached an [9]*unacceptable* level.

[10]*Regards*,

Ben Southgate

2 Look at words and phrases 1–10 in the e-mail and write the numbers next to the correct feature of formal e-mails.

Formal greeting	_____
Using full forms, not contractions	_____ _____
Formal words and expressions	_____ _____ _____ _____
Passives to avoid being personal	_____ _____
Formal ending	_____

3 Order the letters to form nouns to complete the sentences. What is the verb form of each noun?

1 The dressing rooms need a lot of i_____. NTPRMOEVME

2 Gym members need better instructions to avoid i_____. RUJNY

3 Prices are already high. An i_____ is unreasonable. RENCASE

4 Changes to class schedules have caused c_____. NFUONOSI

5 The m_____ should run the gym more efficiently. NTNAGAEME

6 We are not given enough i_____ about how to use the equipment safely. NFROAMITNO

7 The d_____ that we were being given dirty towels was shocking. COVISERY

8 I have made the d_____ to cancel my membership. ISCENOI

9 Your plan to raise the price came as an unwelcome s_____. REURPSI

4 You have received an e-mail telling you that the cost of your gym membership is going up. You feel this is unreasonable because of the poor quality of the gym. Write a formal e-mail of complaint.

• Include three paragraphs: say why you are writing, explain the situation, and say what you want to be done.

• Use the features of formal e-mails in exercise 2.

• Use the sentences in exercise 3 for ideas.

78

WRITING PRACTICE

WRITING: Making writing interesting

1 Read Eva's description of her first meeting with her neighbor. Choose the correct words to complete the text.

The first time I met Davina, I was very <u>scared</u> of her! It was only the second day in my apartment when she knocked on my door to complain that I was being too <u>noisy</u>. ¹*However / As well / Although* it was two o'clock in the afternoon, she was wearing a pair of pajamas with a huge old black coat on top. Her long blonde hair was sticking up all over the place. She looked really <u>sleepy</u>, and really <u>angry</u>, ²*too / also / however*.

She told me she was a nurse and she was trying to sleep ³*because / so / that's why* she had been working all night. ⁴*But / That's why / And* she was wearing pajamas. Of course, I apologized. I suddenly realized how <u>loud</u> my music was ⁵*because / too / so* I wasn't surprised she was <u>annoyed</u>.

I felt really bad. ⁶*Although / That's why / However*, the next day a card was slid under my door, inviting me for coffee on the weekend. That's when I discovered that Davina is really a lovely person when she's not <u>tired</u>!

Now we get along really well. We sometimes go out together, and I ⁷*also / as well / too* take care of her friendly little brown and white cat when she goes out of town. Of course, I'm not <u>frightened</u> of her any more, ⁸*but / because / also* I never play loud music now!

2 Look at the <u>underlined</u> words in Eva's description and make four pairs of synonyms.

3 Look at the adjectives in these sentences. Write them in the correct columns.

1 My roommate is a **lovely young Italian** woman.
2 We sat at a **big round wood** table.
3 Milo had **beautiful long brown** hair.
4 Hannah was wearing a **blue cotton** shirt.
5 Chris has a **fat old black** dog.
6 Karl cooks **delicious French** food.

opinion	size	shape	age	colour	nationality	material

4 Write about the first time you met someone you have a relationship with now, for example, a neighbor, friend, colleague, or roommate.

- Use interesting adjectives, in the correct order, to describe things.
- Use synonyms to avoid repeating words.
- Use linkers to give reasons and results (*so, because, that's why*), to contrast information (*but, although, however*) or add information (*and, also, too, as well*).

NOTES

NOTES

NOTES

NOTES

NOTES

Richmond

58 St Aldates
Oxford
OX1 1ST
United Kingdom

Second reprint: 2023
ISBN: 978-84-668-2690-7

© Richmond / Santillana Global S.L. 2018

All rights reserved. No part of this book may be reproduced, stored in a retrieval system or transmitted in any form by any means, electronic, mechanical, photocopying, recording or otherwise, without the prior permission in writing of the Publisher.

Publishing Director: Deborah Tricker

Publisher: Simone Foster

Media Publisher: Sue Ashcroft

Workbook Publisher: Luke Baxter

Content Developer: David Cole-Powney

Editors: Debra Emmett, Helen Ward, Ruth Cox, Emma Clarke, Fiona Hunt, Eleanor Clements, Helen Wendholt

Proofreaders: Peter Anderson, Jamie Bowman, Tas Cooper, Fiona Hunt, Amanda Leigh

Design Manager: Lorna Heaslip

Cover Design: This Ain't Rock'n'Roll, London

Design & Layout: Lorna Heaslip, Oliver Hutton, Gabriela Alvarez

Photo Researcher: Magdalena Mayo

Learning Curve video: Mannic Media

Audio production: Eastern Sky Studios

App development: The Distance

Americanization: Diane Hermanson

We would also like to thank the following people for their valuable contribution to writing and developing the material:
Alastair Lane, Bob McLarty, Claire Thacker, Louis Rogers, Rachael Roberts, Pamela Vittorio (Video Script Writer), Belen Fernandez (App Project Manager), Rob Sved (App Content Creator)

Illustrators:
Simon Clare; Dermot Flynn c/o Dutch Uncle; Guillaume Gennet, Julien Kern and Liav Zabari c/o Lemonade; Joanna Kerr c/o New Division; Piers Sandford c/o Meiklejohn; The Boy FitzHammond and Beverley Young, c/o NB Illustration

Photos:
J. Jaime; J. Lucas; 123RF/ lightpoet; ALAMY/IanDagnall Laptop Computing, John Birdsall, Chuck Place, Granger Historical Picture Archve, All Canada Photos, Cofiant Images, ONOKY - Photononstop, Action Plus Sports Images, Arcaid Images, Jasminko Ibrakovic, Image Source Salsa, Radius Images, Pat Behnke, Ann Cutting, 360b, Heritage Image Partnership Ltd, Roger Bamber, Cultura Creative (RF), Blend Images, RosalreneBetancourt 10, Nick Gregory, BSIP SA, Trinity Mirror / Mirrorpix, Wavebreak Media ltd, Torontonian, Joy Sunny, SWNS, TP, IanDagnall Computing, PhotoEdit, Ammentorp Photography, Peter Barritt, Cliff Hide Stock, greenwales, caia image, eye35.pix, Carlos Guerra, Janine Wiedel Photolibrary, Peter Titmuss, Richard Heyes, Motoring Picture Library, Helen Hotson, Cephas Picture Library, ACORN 1, tommaso altamura, Steve Davey Photography, Image Source, Bill Cheyrou, Agencja Fotograficzna Caro, Kreative Photography, Imagedoc, Lou-Foto, Julie g Woodhouse, allesalltag, Stefano Carvoretto, MAX EAREY, wareham.nl (sport), Duncan Snow, Wilawan Khasawong, Brian Overcast, Design Pics Inc, Westend61 GmbH, Anton Stariskov, Elina Manninen, Aflo Co., Ltd., Alan Smith, Classic Image, Photos 12, D. Hurst, MBI, AF archive, PjrTravel, FineArt, moodboard, DonSmith, Jeramey Lende, epa european pressphoto agency b.v.;
BNPS (BOURNEMOUTH NEWS & PICTURE SERVICE)/ Rijksmuseum/ BNPS; CATERS NEWS AGENCY/ Caters News Agency; GETTY IMAGES SALES SPAIN/Lumi Images/Dario Secen, Graham Monro/gm photographics, Jetta Productions, Thomas_EyeDesign, Photos.com Plus, David M. Benett, Astrid Stawiarz, Mark Metcalfe, CARL DE SOUZA, Alistair Berg, Toby Burrows, Sam Edwards, Dave Hogan, Barcroft, Maskot, Bloomberg, Bettmann, Don Arnold, Kari Lehr, PETER MACDIARMID, RENE SLAMA, Boston Globe, CHRISTOPHE ARCHAMBAULT, Caiaimage/Paul Bradbury, Image source, Paul Chesley, Thinkstock; HIGHRES PRESS STOCK/AbleStock.com; ISTOCKPHOTO/SeanShot, Pali Rao, oztasbc, jojoo64, SondraP, MollyNZ, Geber86, xijian, vgajic, sturti, olaser, miralex, mergez, alexsl, HASLOO, SolStock, DONOT6, Getty Images Sales Spain, Devasahayam Chandra Dhas, monkeybusinessimages, Osmany Torres Martín, alessandroguerriero, AleksandarGeorgiev, Tommaso Altamura, Nicolas McComber, warrengoldswain, travellinglight, stevecoleimages, Robyn Mackenzie, German-skydiver, digitalskillet, Wavebreakmedia, Petar Chernaev, Jaroslav Frank, wundervisuals, Squaredpixels, LuckyBusiness, Julia Nichols, Drazen Lovric, Dean Mitchell, elenaleonova, PeopleImages, Elenathewise, Dieter Meyrl, Daniel Ernst, Cathy Yeulet, ozgurdonmaz, mediaphotos, Yuri_Arcurs, Visiofutura, Jason Poole, David Sucsy, Bulent Ince, nataistock, bluehill75, calvindexter, MartialRed, Juanmonino, FangXiaNuo, Joel Carillet, FSTOPLIGHT, DeluXe-PiX, DeanDrobot, g-stockstudio, zhudifeng, pixdeluxe, milanfoto, dolgachov, cindygoff, SteveTram, OcusFocus, robertcicchetti, Maxiphoto, Kaan Ates, Huchen Lu, Anna Bryukhanova, Halfpoint, CactuSoup, yipengge, mihailomilovanovic, urbancow, rcaucino, pepifoto, lucky336, kyoshino, denphumi; MAYANG MURNI ADNIN; NASA/ NASA; REX SHUTTERSTOCK/Jonathan Player, ABC Inc/ Everett, Peter Brooker, Kippa Limited, Pixelformula, Newspix; SHUTTERSTOCK; SHUTTERSTOCK NETHERLANDS,B.V.; Project Jacquard/Levi's Strauss; Library of Congress/wikipedia; Carpigiani Gelato University; Niccolo Casas /EMBR labs; Optomen Television Ltd.; courtesy of Alex Deans; Pauline Van Dongen; Alastair Humphreys; freepic.com; Ringly Inc.; Jon Barlow; Dave Homcy; ALAMY/Frances Roberts, Nick Baylis, REUTERS, David Taylor, Paul Nichols, Mode Images, M L Pearson, Jeremey Richards, Panther Media GmBH, Big Cheese Photo LLC, Digital Image Library, Sabena Jane Blackbird, www.BibleLandPictures. com, Purcell Team; GETTY IMAGES SALES SPAIN/ Thinkstock; ISTOCKPHOTO/Getty Images Sales Spain; REX SHUTTERSTOCK/Solent News; ARCHIVO SANTILLANA; Images used under licence from ©Shutterstock.com

Cover Photo: Jon Barlow

We would like to thank the following reviewers for their valuable feedback which has made Personal Best possible. We extend our thanks to the many teachers and students not mentioned here.

Brad Bawtinheimer, Manuel Hidalgo, Paulo Dantas, Diana Bermúdez, Laura Gutiérrez, Hardy Griffin, Angi Conti, Christopher Morabito, Hande Kokce, Jorge Lobato, Leonardo Mercato, Mercilinda Ortiz, Wendy López

The Publisher has made every effort to trace the owner of copyright material; however, the Publisher will correct any involuntary omission at the earliest opportunity.

Impressão e acabamento:
A.S. Pereira Gráfica e Editora EIRELI
Lote: 796.384   Código: 290526907
2024